Brian Wm. Niles

Overthrowing Dead Culture

A Vision to Change the World of College Recruiting

We started TargetX in 1998 on the idea that there is a growing disconnect between how students search for and select the right college and how colleges communicate with them. Over the past twelve years, the TargetX team has challenged the status quo of college admissions and recruiting through regular speaking engagements, blogging, tweeting, podcasting, and webcasting in an endless pursuit to reduce this disconnect and help our clients succeed and prosper in the new world of college admissions.

This book, *Overthrowing Dead Culture*, is a culmination of that effort to date. And while my name is on it, it has come together thanks to the talent and dedication of the TargetX team. While our clients get to work with these wonderful folks on an occasional basis, I get to work with them every day.

I couldn't imagine doing it with anyone else.

We hope you enjoy reading *Overthrowing Dead Culture*.

I welcome your feedback to me personally

at niles@targetx.com. Best wishes and peace.

—Brian Wm. Niles, CEO

Summer 2010

Contents

1

The Problem

*There is a growing disconnect between how colleges recruit students
and how students search for the right-fit college.*
—TargetX Vision Statement, 1998

There's a price to pay when you resist change—and it's a big one for college leaders who preside over archaic admissions cultures that don't connect with twenty-first century students and families.

Consider Digital Equipment Corp., the industry leader in mid-range computers in the early 1990s. The company isn't around today for one good reason—it didn't foresee the ascent of the personal computer. "There is no reason anyone would want a computer in their home," said Ken Olson, president, chairman, and founder of Digital in 1977.

Digital isn't alone. There are other formerly brand-name companies that aren't in business today because their hidebound cultures couldn't or wouldn't adapt to changing conditions in their industry.

Western Union had a chance to *own* the telephone but passed. In 1876, Alexander Graham Bell, inventor of the telephone, offered his telephone patent to Western-Union for $100,000. Their reply? "This 'telephone' has too many shortcomings to be seriously considered as a means of communication. The device is inherently of no value to us," said a Western-Union internal memo. History hasn't been kind to Western-Union's reply. The telephone patent has been estimated as the most valuable patent of all time. Ironically, Bell's company, AT&T, later acquired Western-Union.

Royal and Underwood typewriters were once the industry leaders. But when company executives scoffed at the notion of electronic typewriters and word processors, the companies clearly weren't ready for the age of the computer chip. By the late 1970s, the companies were out of business.

In 1950, Great Britain made 80 percent of the world's motorcycles. Today it makes less than 1 percent. U.K.-based Triumph, the former leader in motorcycle manufacturing, kept using outdated and inefficient production methods while counterparts like Japan's Honda and the U.S.'s Harley-Davidson turned to cheaper, modernized production methods—and basically put Triumph out of business.

Will today's colleges suffer the same fate? No, certainly not all of them. But colleges that don't adapt to rapid, revolutionary changes in higher education and that don't adapt with an authentic, technology-based message to students and families will go the way of Digital, Western-Union, and Royal Typewriter—out of business.

The second decade of the twenty-first century brings a new collegiate landscape, one forged from the greatest economic downturn in the past eighty years but one also forged from a decades-long revolution in technology that has permanently changed the ways students want to communicate with colleges.

The last time we bore witness to such immense change was fifty years ago when U.S. colleges enjoyed a bull market in enrollment. Then, high school students began viewing the collegiate experience as easily attainable, if not a birthright. Shielded from the military draft and drawn by highly affordable tuition rates, American high school students landed on college campuses in droves.

Steven P. Dresch, writing in the *Academy of Political Science* ("College Enrollment," 1983), points out that collegiate enrollment had meandered along from 1880 to 1960 but with a slow, steady rate of growth: "Between 1880 and 1960, the college age population (consisting of persons between the ages of 18–24) increased at an annual rate of 1.1 percent. During the same period, however, college enrollment grew at an annual rate of 4.4 percent." But in the decade starting in 1960, Dresch shows that the rate of college enrollment doubled the previous eighty-years' rate of growth—all in one ten-year period: "The growth rate of the college-aged population increased to 4.2 percent, while the rate of enrollment growth surged to more than 8.0 percent."

Then, as now, changing economic conditions (for the better in the case of the 1960s) and shifting demographics (especially a rise in incomes in lower- and middle-class American families) paved the way for millions of high school students to hit U.S. collegiate campuses by storm. For the past fifty years, the college experience has been a highly viable option for a high percentage of U.S. high school students.

Those days are over. Now, tens of millions of U.S. parents who have seen their home values plummet and their investment accounts drained can no longer afford the average cost of even one year of college. While Americans' financial fortunes are in decline, college costs keep rising. In 2009, the average tuition at four-year public colleges rose 6.5 percent, or $429, to $7,020, according to the College Board's annual "Trends in College Pricing" report. At private colleges, the average list price for a year of course work rose 4.4 percent to $26,273. Those numbers don't even account for room, board, and other expenses.

An Unsustainable Truth

According to the biennial report titled "Measuring Up" (2008), from the National Center for Public Policy and Higher Education, the rising cost of college threatens to put higher education out of reach for most Americans. The center's president, Patrick M. Callan, said, "If we go on this way for another 25 years, we won't have an affordable system of higher education."

Tough Times for Colleges

U.S. colleges have seen their endowments fall by 23 percent since 2007. In the September 2009 edition of *Time*, the magazine lists several unique ways that colleges and universities are coping with a sustained, slumping economy—to the point of counting nickels and dimes. Here are some examples:

- Bryn Mawr College saved $900 by holding a virtual swim meet and thus cutting travel costs.

- Dickinson College dropped its free laundry service, saving $150,000.

- Carleton College saved $3,800 by not serving shrimp and wine at its annual faculty parties.

- Pitzer College saved $80,000 by power-washing the sidewalks only once each year.

Economic Impact of the Great Recession on Colleges

There is no doubt that colleges are caught between two eras. Behind them are decades of traditions and tenets that have historically served colleges well in their search for new students to share the unique experience that each campus offers. In front of them is the second decade of the twenty-first century, which poses challenges in the form of a troubled economy and new modes of communication that schools have failed—or are at least reluctant—to master.

Perhaps the most troubling element is the sliding U.S. economy, which shows all the signs of changing the college recruiting admissions landscape for the long term—and decidedly downward.

Call it a tipping point or even the "new normal." For the economy, in general, and the college financial environment, in particular, the numbers tell the story. Things have changed—and they won't be changing back anytime soon.

To understand how these changes impact college admissions, let's start by understanding the factors inhibiting the U.S. economy:

- As of 2009, government figures show that U.S. revolving consumer debt, made up almost entirely of credit card debt, was about $950 billion. In the fourth quarter of 2008, 13.9 percent of consumer disposable income went to service this debt.

- The U.S. Government debt has increased by over two trillion dollars in 2009 alone, according to the U.S. Congressional Budget Office. Consider that, as of 2009, 100 percent of GDP was around $13 trillion. Putting things into context, before the Great Depression in 1929, the U.S. government debt was only 15 percent of GDP.

- Factor in a complete mispricing of money, along with some flashy financial innovations, which led to the housing boom and allowed buyers to purchase homes with no down payments and homeowners to refinance their existing mortgages.

- Add to the mix a consumption boom, which wasn't matched, at least here in the United States, by an equal amount of industrial production and capital spending increases.

- All of this caused the U.S. trade deficit to expand and the current-account deficit to expand from 2 percent of GDP in 1998 to approximately 7 percent in mid-2009 (and it is still rising).

These trends—no longer singular forces—speckle the economic landscape like a plague, creating a toxic economic stew that could, and probably will, lead to a significantly lower standard of living for debt-ravaged Americans. Make no mistake, that also includes the great American middle class, academia's traditional source for millions of potential college students.

The College Endowment Calamity

Naturally, bad news in the U.S. economy bleeds into every nook and cranny of the U.S. economy, including the market for higher learning institutions (and, as I'll describe in this book, it is a highly competitive market).

Nowhere is this more crystal clear than in the college endowment environment. Endowments are a powerful financial force in higher education, with many individual college endowments totaling $1 billion or more.

But the economy hasn't treated the collegiate endowment market well in the past few years. By and large, the endowment boom peaked in 2007. At that point, the average return on U.S. college endowments was 17 percent—significantly ahead of the 12 percent returned by the Standard & Poor's 500 index over the past fifty years.

But by mid-2008, the high-flying endowment market had crash landed. The economic crisis had a stranglehold on the financial market and endowments were no exception. By the end of the year, the average U.S. collegiate endowment was down 23 percent for the year, before regaining some stability in 2009. But school administrators were still left to deal with a stunning blow—about a quarter of their direct financial resources had evaporated and weren't coming back soon, if at all.

> "The fallout [was] fast and furious," said *Institutional Investor* magazine ("U.S. colleges are forced to re-evaluate their endowment models," November 4, 2009).

> "Hundreds of universities across the U.S. have put building projects on hold, closed classes, fired staff, frozen salaries and scaled back benefits. Harvard, for example, eliminated 275 jobs this year in addition to halting construction in Allston. Yale reduced staff salaries and other non-personnel costs by 12.5 percent and froze several hundred job vacancies. Princeton, which chose to skip a transfer of funds from its endowment to its operating budget last spring, convinced 145 staff members to take early retirement as part of a two-year, $170 million (13 percent) budget cut and is now facing further staff reductions. Stanford has laid off 412 staff members, and 60 more people will lose their jobs by the end of the year."

Due to the huge endowment losses suffered by colleges and universities, and the subsequent decline in donations from alumni, who were also adversely impacted by the global recession, schools were forced to do the unthinkable—issue bonds to raise much-needed cash.

> "Harvard was first, floating $1.5 billion in taxable bonds last December, joined early this year by Princeton and Stanford, which each issued $1 billion in bonds," said *Institutional Investor*. "By the time most students had

gone home for summer break, Brown University, the University of Chicago, Cornell University, Duke University, Johns Hopkins University and Vanderbilt University had followed suit, issuing anywhere from $100 million to $500 million in bonds."

Public Colleges Losing Government Funding

The economic malaise that colleges are experiencing couldn't have come at a worse time. Right now, there are over 4,000 colleges and universities in the United States—and they're all competing for about 3.3 million high school students, according to a study by the College Board. Other studies say that number is higher. The National Center for Education Statistics predicted that by 2010, more than 9,000,000 students will attend college full-time in the United States, up from 5,000,000 in 1970.

But those numbers could be deceiving. Studies also show that there is mixed interest on the part of high school kids to go to college. Many opt to go straight into the workforce, or attend college via online courses. And the kids who do go on to college are increasingly forced, mostly due to economic reasons, to attend cheaper public colleges and universities.

Even so, public universities have their own financial problems. The amount of public funding such schools receive from their respective states is in decline. In Virginia, public funding for state colleges has declined from 30 percent (of total university funding) in the 1980s to 8 percent today. It's the same story in Wisconsin, where funding over the same time frame is down from 30 percent to 19 percent—and these are states with impressive public colleges

Endowments Falling For Private Colleges

According to the U.S. Department of Education, endowments account for 13 percent of private-college budgets—compared to 2 percent for public college budgets.

and universities. That has forced state schools to raise tuition rates to make up the difference, thus further eroding demand from potential enrollees.

Perhaps even worse, colleges are really beginning to turn off students and their families. If colleges don't understand that the rules are changing—and by *rules* I mean changing demographics, economic uncertainty, and technology that levels the playing field and gives families more control than ever over the college admissions process—then parents sure do. They want colleges to meet them halfway—an option that schools historically have been leery of if not outright resistant to, doing. Take this actual letter from a parent, explaining to Northeastern University why the school priced itself out of his child's school choice options.

Dear Admissions Person:

First, let me open by saying thank you on behalf of Alex for his acceptance to Northeastern University—clearly an outstanding university. Next, I wanted to let you know that he will not be attending Northeastern, having chosen to attend the University of Connecticut instead. The main reason for his decision is one of economics—approximately $20K per year total cost at UConn vs. $47K per year total cost at Northeastern.

Over the past few years it has become increasingly clear that private universities such as Northeastern are pricing the middle class out of attending their schools. With the rising cost of tuition and room and board far outstripping increases in cost of living, you are basically closing the doors to all but the wealthy, who have no problem paying the total cost of attending college no matter what that cost is, or the underprivileged students who have achieved academically, yet have no way to pay for a college education. The main question is, could we afford to pay for Alex to attend Northeastern having been offered very little to no financial aid? The answer is yes, IF we chose to take thousands of dollars in loans, tap into our retirement funds, and use the equity that we've built in our home. All completely unreasonable expectations by universities such as yours. The next question: Is an undergraduate degree from Northeastern worth (4 × $27K) $108K more than an undergraduate degree from UConn? The answer clearly is absolutely not. In fact, the general population is now beginning to see more clearly that where the undergrad degree is earned, provided that it's from an accredited institution, is not really as critical as institutions of higher learning want them to believe. Also, the major marketing effort (mailings, calls) that Northeastern has engaged in with accepted students leads me to believe that your admissions rate may be lower than you expected this academic year.

So, with little financial aid from Northeastern to bring your costs in line with what Alex has been offered by UConn and based on his decision that your costs are far too high, he has decided to accept admission to UCONN, majoring in physiology and neurobiology for the 2009–2010 academic year.

Sincerely,
Robert—

Demographic Challenges

It's not just parents who stand in the way of colleges' long-term structural health—it's the high-school-age sons and daughters of those parents, too.

The economy has something to do with that, as does the advent of technology and the Internet. All of these factors are contributing to a changing face of college admissions as we enter the second decade of the twenty-first century.

In a June 2009 study by the National Association for College Admission Counseling (NACAC), we can see how the economy is shifting the landscape for colleges and universities—especially those higher-end schools that historically only had to hang an *open for business* sign out on the front gate and watch the students and the money roll in.

Among the highlights of the survey:

- A significant minority of public (37.6 percent) and private (40.1 percent) high schools reported more applications per student, but a plurality for both sectors reported that the application-per-student ratio (which many feared might rise significantly this year) was about the same as last year.

- Interest in community colleges was up, especially at public high schools, 62.9 percent of which reported an increase in the number of students selecting community colleges; only 2.9 percent reported a decrease. Among private high schools, most counseling officials reported no change in interest in community colleges, but 21.3 percent saw more students going to two-year institutions.

- Solid majorities at both public and private high schools reported a shift in enrollment patterns, with an increase in those enrolling in public colleges.

- Solid majorities at both public and private high schools reported that more students this year than in the past were not enrolling at their dream schools for economic reasons.

- Public colleges were more likely to see their yields (the percentage of accepted applicants who enroll) go up, while the opposite was true for private colleges.

- Significant minorities of public and private colleges saw increases in the percentages of students accepted through early decision who declined to enroll, citing inadequate financial aid.

The tables that follow show how the NACAC study numbers break down. Note the upward shift into community colleges and public colleges and away from private colleges and universities.

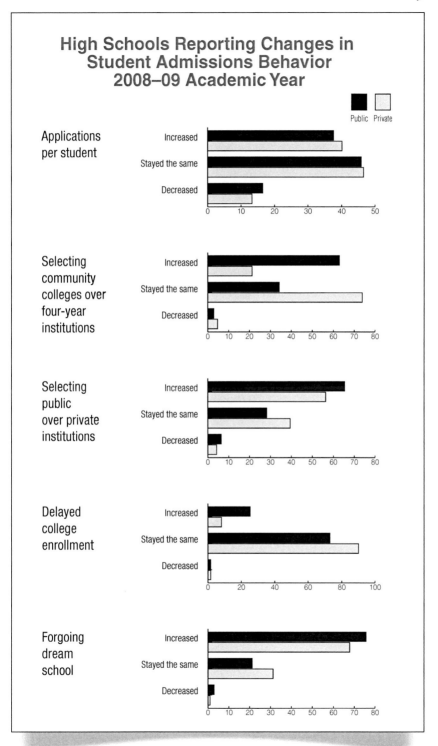

High Schools Reporting Changes in Student Admissions Behavior 2008–09 Academic Year

Public Private

Applications per student
- Increased
- Stayed the same
- Decreased

0   10   20   30   40   50

Selecting community colleges over four-year institutions
- Increased
- Stayed the same
- Decreased

0   10   20   30   40   50   60   70   80

Selecting public over private institutions
- Increased
- Stayed the same
- Decreased

0   10   20   30   40   50   60   70   80

Delayed college enrollment
- Increased
- Stayed the same
- Decreased

0   20   40   60   80   100

Forgoing dream school
- Increased
- Stayed the same
- Decreased

0   10   20   30   40   50   60   70   80

Source: National Association for College Admissions Counseling.

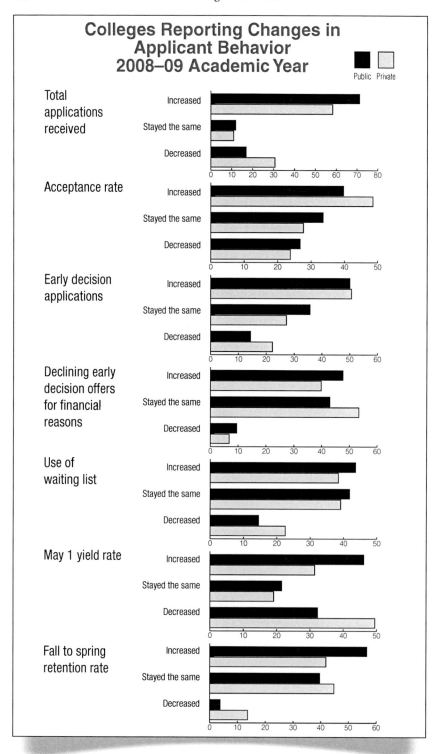

Source: National Association for College Admissions Counseling.

The NACAC study increasingly demonstrates that recent demographic and economic trends have created a buyer's market for students in lieu of the seller's market that colleges have enjoyed for decades.

But it's not just economics. In a major way, technology and communications have bypassed the way that colleges have reached out to potential students. In the days when glossy marketing packages arrived in their parents' mailboxes, it was colleges that called the shots; it was admissions offices that dictated how schools and students would communicate; and it was admissions offices that led students and families around by the nose, directing how applications would be handled, how finances would be covered, and how marketing campaigns would be delivered.

But the Internet changed all that. As websites proliferated and technology went mobile in the form of cell phones and laptop computers with WiFi access, gradually it was the students who started setting the terms.

I've devoted an entire chapter in this book to how technology has completely changed the college admissions landscape, but suffice it to say that if colleges really want to understand high school students, they should spend less time developing slick brochures and viewbooks and spend more time on Facebook, or Google, and on their own websites. Conversations take place on Facebook. Google is the new student search.

These economic and technological shifts have caused significant changes that include savvier students, more price-conscious moms and dads, and a downshift in budgets as reduced endowments and lower charitable funding could easily translate into less expensive adjunct instructors, online and Internet courses, and, quite possibly, fewer students and less revenue. Simultaneously, students and parents, challenged by a sustained economic downturn, will likely turn to options that were unheard of ten years ago, such as community college or even deferring enrollment by a year or more.

Make no mistake, these are the lean times, not only for American families but for colleges and universities, too.

Can Colleges Change Their "Dead Culture?"

The Northeastern letter writer I cited earlier, like a lot of college-age kids, and thier parents, realizes something that many colleges don't. The system is broken, and they want it fixed.

Right now. Not next year.

The result of all of these challenges—and it's one of the best-kept secrets in academia—is that colleges and universities have little margin for error.

Considering the dramatic decline in college financial funds, can colleges overthrow "dead culture" and right themselves before it's too late?

From my position as co founder and CEO of TargetX, a leading interactive collegiate recruiting firm in the United States, and from my twenty years manning the front lines of the college admissions battlefield, I have a unique perspective on what works and what doesn't in the university recruitment marketplace.

Of course, I have a wonderful, talented group at TargetX who've been invaluable in helping me get that perspective—and use it to help colleges shed that "dead culture" and start the process of changing their admissions programs to attract good students to their campuses.

Rooted in the 1970s

Archaic recruitment strategies—like most ideas whose time has come and passed—often inflict the worst damage on the very people the strategies are trying to help. Today's admissions culture, for example, has led to students applying to multiple colleges, even going so far as to pay multiple deposits, and triggering more paperwork in what is growing into a Byzantine college admissions process. It's a process that still seems rooted in the 1970s, when high school students chose one or maybe two (read safe) colleges to attend. It's an expansion of the same process where the criteria are based on benchmarks, expectations, and assumptions that serve neither the university—or the student and his or her family well.

Fast Fact

In a study by Longmire and Company, 40 percent of respondents said that economic changes in the last few years had negatively impacted their plans for college. Twenty percent of that group said they will give more weight to cheaper community colleges or colleges closer to home.

Unfortunately, the staid, inadequate ways that colleges market themselves to students and families—at least the ways students and families *expect* colleges to market admissions services to them—aren't working anymore.

Viewbooks, mass marketing, carnival-like college fairs, confused campus visits hosted by disinterested collegians who are given a script and have a habit of making the least of it—all are key cornerstones of today's college admissions marketing programs, and they all have major cracks in the façade.

Perhaps unbeknownst to college educators, such programs only serve to muddy the waters even further—they confuse students and families and cause a gap between what families want and what universities provide via the admissions marketing process. It's the collegiate equivalent of playing the kids' swimming pool game "Marco Polo." Everybody's blindly talking past each other and nobody's connecting, leaving both sides dissatisfied with the way students are recruited. With little rhyme and no reason, universities have created disparate models of admitting students. No matter the perceived quality of the college or university, colleges use constantly revolving criteria and reasoning to decide which students get accepted, why they're accepted, and how the college will invest its admissions marketing resources.

Even worse, the vehicles used by colleges to tout their educational experiences, that is, their "brands," are outmoded and inadequate. In the age of online search and social networking, where cultural icons like Facebook and Google have a vicelike grip on the consciousness of young Americans, colleges still send out mass market mailers, similar to how Ford made Edsels long after the demands by American consumers for such vehicles had waned. Students don't read the mailers and, more and more, parents have come to view them with suspicion (and they may look like junk mail).

Equally archaic are the ubiquitous viewbooks colleges use to display their campuses and cultures in a glossy, eight-by-ten package—once again, that few students and parents ever read. Not sure of their footing with students, colleges have also started sending their mass marketing materials to families early in the recruitment process—sometimes as early as the student's sophomore year in high school (not a bad idea in theory, just in the way it's currently executed).

All in all, today's admissions culture is a wounded one—I would say mortally so—and it needs to change.

Looking at Change from the Inside Out

With the online era, interactive recruiting is all about change.

Change is a mantra that I use all the time when I speak to college administrators—I'm forever beseeching them not to be afraid of change. After all, change provides us with new opportunities. With the invention of the magnetic compass, Columbus was able to sail across the Atlantic. Prior to the compass, ships had to stay close to land. And, as Heraclitus said five hundred years before the birth of Christ, "the only permanent thing is change."

In other words, change is inevitable. Consider the railroad, which replaced the lumbering Conestoga wagons that transported freight across U.S. prairies. Or how about telegraphs, which originally sprouted along railroad lines? Soon they gave way to the telephone, which in turn is giving way to wireless communication.

At the end of the nineteenth century, Americans bore witness to the motorized automobile. An aberration at first, automobiles soon dotted newly constructed urban roads and highways. After seeing the glories of automotive travel, Americans no longer had a need for a horse and buggy. So it goes with gasoline lamps giving way to electricity and the typewriter giving way to the personal computer. Good ideas in their day, all giving way to better ones. So, it's no surprise that the death of the college admissions process, was also imminent. Obviously (to me, anyway) admissions programs couldn't have gone on forever, could they? Like other cultural supernovas like the steam engine and the horse and buggy, the old ways of recruiting kids to campus had to give way to better ideas.

Finding the Right Formula

As a result of changing economic conditions and a competitive college admissions environment, it's not just a question of high school students wanting to attend college. It is, as Lloyd Thacker writes in *College Unranked: Affirming Educational Values in College Admissions*, a question of "attending the right college."

That's not so easy, especially in the demographic and economic environment discussed earlier in the chapter—especially relating to colleges and universities. After years of steady increase, the number of graduating high school students in the country has peaked. Projections show that the number of graduates will now decrease until around 2015. For colleges and universities that means, coupled with the shortfall in family budgets, the high demand of the last few years will shrink as fewer and fewer students apply. Competition between schools will increase; students will have more options and more power in the application process.

> **Fast Fact**
>
> According to the College Board, college marketing spending is growing at a rate of 5–10 percent annually—exceeding $1.5 billion in 2007.

This shift in the playing field will force many colleges and universities to make a long delayed adjustment in their recruiting efforts. As other industries moved on to more modern technologies to broadcast themselves in a rapidly evolving world, higher education has for the most part remained in the past, relying on the same old methods of reaching prospective applicants.

That approach was adequate—if not exceptional—during a period when more and more students were looking to postsecondary education. With the job pool for high school graduates shrinking at the same time, schools had the upper hand when it came to determining how the application process worked. Students had to play along or fall behind the competition—and a "dead culture" continued to work for most schools' bottom lines.

But what happens when school officials wake up one day and find that applicants aren't knocking down their doors to get in? Will students still be willing to jump through the same hoops and settle for the same recruiting games?

Let's say you're a high school student in the year 2012. You do well in school, enough to gain entrance to most of the better colleges and universities in the country. Like most teenagers, you also live through your technology. Your iPod, cell phone, and laptop computer aren't just fancy appliances; they're your portals to the world around you.

Now take a moment to observe the students at your institution. They, too, use technology for fun and socializing. But they also use it for work. They take notes on their laptops in class. They use online databases and programs to study and do projects. Some of their teachers may even record lectures for the students to listen to later on their iPods. Technology isn't just for leisure; it's become fully integrated into their lives.

The point is, technology doesn't decrease in importance after high school. Rather, it becomes even more pervasive, more sophisticated, and more important to a student's education.

So why do colleges and universities continue to act as though, somewhere in between those two stages, a student will respond to recruiting efforts that woefully fail to reach out to or even acknowledge this relationship?

NACAC Survey: Dream Colleges... Up In Smoke?

According to the NACAC, a majority (70 percent) of high schools reported an increase in the number of students who felt the need to modify their ambitions and choose more affordable options over their "dream schools." Says NACAC: "The reverberations of a shaky economy were also felt on the college side, as 45 percent of colleges reported a decrease in the number of students accepting admission offers, also known as yield rates in the admissions office, compared to 2008. The survey also found that 35 percent of the reporting colleges experienced budget cuts."

Instead they produce generic, halfhearted brochures and mailings that broadcast the same stiff, corporate messages that today's media-savvy teenagers instinctively distrust. For most of today's students, a brochure is something they find in their dentist's waiting room or their school's main office—it's *usually* boring, it's static and it provides only the most basic information. Simply put, it's the complete opposite of what today's instant gratification technology has conditioned them to expect. It's what we call "talk-at" marketing.

The way these print publications are distributed is also a completely alien convention in today's teenager's customized, instant access world. Thousands of brochures— each one no different from the other—stamped with the student's formal name and address, and dropped off in the mail with the rest of the junk mail and cheesy catalogues. The procedure is not only glacial and totally impractical in an age when information is shared instantaneously online, but it also sends a message to students: We don't think like you think.

The growing divide between the evolutionary paths of print and web media is a good starting point for a look into the separate thinking of students and postsecondary schools when it comes to recruiting.

A Labored Applications Process

It's not just about unwanted or unread marketing materials.

We know from the research we've done at TargetX that students believe most schools are behind the times in their application materials. The other reality we've found— one perhaps obscured by the steady rise in college applications over the past few years—is that students also dislike the application process in the first place.

In a recent report by the Education Conservancy, interviewed students expressed frustration with the ambiguity of the application process. They felt schools were not giving direct, honest information about what they wanted from applicants.

Most important, the report went on to find that students distrusted schools' recruiting efforts. They saw the marketing campaigns as hollow, ineffectual attempts to make colleges seem unique or tailored to the student being recruited. They disliked schools' impersonal appeals for students to apply even when it was clear they would not be admitted. *And worst of all, students did not like the generic way in which institutions conducted their recruiting efforts.* Print mailings, college fairs and informational sessions weren't just seen as outdated; they were considered sales pitches—just the school trying to make another buck.

Up until the great economic calamity at the end of the first decade of the twenty-first century, colleges and universities were sheltered from the repercussions of these critiques because of inflated demand. Students could complain all they wanted as long as they kept applying in droves—which they did. And the schools continued to adhere to the old, outdated recruiting formula, even as it gradually chipped away at the tenuous relationships they had with each successive application class.

Let's go back to the high school student in the year 2012. It's application time, and she is beginning to put together her search. She has some ideas about what she wants in her future college, but she is also relying on the colleges to reach out to her.

Brochures begin cluttering her mailbox. Her high school starts to host college visits and informational sessions. Her guidance counselor advises her to schedule visits to prospective schools.

But the whole process is too slow. She is used to instant information. Rather than wait for mailings or face-to-face interviews that could take weeks to arrange, she does what's natural: She Googles. She emails. She goes online to find whatever she can, as fast as she can.

And what does she find? Most likely an assemblage of schools that are wholly unprepared for this cyber outreach. She quickly grows impatient with websites that are bland, interchangeable, and intent on highlighting information and features she doesn't care about. She gets cookie-cutter email responses from college recruiters essentially telling her to go back to the traditional phone call/snail mail route she had been trying to bypass in the first place. And she gets the impression that she and these schools are communicating on totally different wavelengths.

That's the tricky part for colleges—getting up to speed with marketing technology doesn't mean throwing up a halfway decent webpage, sending out waves of mass emails, and calling it a day. Students are online enough to know what separates the good from the bad when it comes to interactivity. Email greetings that come off as spam and websites that look like business Powerpoints are not going to persuade a student that your college is "ahead of the curve." Poor online communication is just going to make you look even more outdated and less in tune with what matters to teenagers.

As the Education Conservancy report showed, students are becoming more cynical of and more attuned to the subtle (and not so subtle) ways colleges market themselves. They are also harder to impress; students interviewed said colleges all sounded the same when they claimed they were unique and different from the rest.

Currently this cultural divide only hurts the student, who is left confused and feeling as though the colleges neither care about nor intend to fix the recruiting mechanisms that seem so stuck in the past. But colleges no longer have the advantage of inflated demand. If they can't effectively market themselves, like any other business, they're not going to survive.

Fast Fact:
Is Print Dead?

In a recent survey by Carnegie Communications, more than half of students polled found web recruitment materials more useful than print brochures, and more than two-thirds thought they provided more in-depth information. In the same poll, students believed about 31 percent of a school's recruiting budget should be invested in its website—a third more than they said should be used for brochures.

Students put even less emphasis on the importance of DVDs and CDs. What student these days is going to pop in that DVD from Byzantine U and spend his valuable free time watching a bland, phony marketing pitch?

And the fact is that most colleges and universities don't have the cachet to survive a failed recruiting effort. For every Harvard or Yale there are countless other schools that have been getting by on the numbers that have been to their advantage. But how is simply playing to strength any way to steel your business for inevitable changes in the marketplace? How does faceless, inaccessible recruiting remain the answer when today's and tomorrow's students demand interactivity and authenticity?

It doesn't.

The only way for colleges to keep afloat in the coming applicant downturn and economic adjustment is to adapt to changing technologies, establish better lines of communication with recruits, and find ways to stand out from the rest of the competition.

Almost all of these goals can be achieved online, using the combined strengths of a school's website, email, and social networking to reach out to that student of the future, who is not looking in her mailbox anymore. Schools hoping to catch up to the online revolution are now starting blogs, setting up Facebook pages, and sending out personalized emails to students. And then there are the podcasts, the virtual campus tours, and the streaming video, all of which broadcast the essential message to students: We're speaking your language.

The Path to Change

Fortunately, there is a way out—but colleges are going to have to grow accustomed to recruiting students differently.

In a word, it's all about attacking college recruiting on multiple fronts: in print, online (via email and websites), through mobile applications (like cell phones), and through improved campus visit experiences. Think of the different approaches as prongs on a fork—they're all different, but they're also tied to one platform—a platform I like to call "interactive" recruiting.

This unique approach to recruitment can help colleges get up to speed and begin fully capitalizing on the efficiency, the accessibility and the effectiveness of interactive recruiting. It's a transition that many schools will find they may not be able to do alone. After all, there is more to schools' seeming refusal to break away from conventional recruiting tactics than stubbornness or ignorance. Many schools simply don't have the resources or the ability to change.

Fast Fact: Demographic Peak?

Though projections vary, according to the *New York Times*, very soon—possibly by the time this book is published—the annual number of U.S. high school students will reach 2.9 million. That's as high as that number has been since the mid-1990s. The *New York Times* adds that we'll see fewer high school students up to and including 2015. Such a scenario would no doubt challenge college admissions officers, who would be looking at a less-than-fertile landscape.

New York Times

But change is essential. You'll see for yourself that interactive recruiting is more than bells and whistles. TargetX's mission isn't to just gloss over your recruiting effort's flaws with flashy graphics and neat interactive features; a full transition from the "dead culture" requires a rebuilding from the ground up. You'll revisit the questions you've been asking recruits, parents and even your own recruiting staff. You'll reevaluate the way your institution makes decisions and markets itself to a generation that has become insulated against marketing. You'll build a recruiting team with the latest technology and recruiting techniques in mind.

More than anything else, you'll discover that interactive recruiting isn't just about what you think students want but about what you *know* they want. Any successful application process needs at its foundation a philosophy that operates on one central premise: students are the ultimate driving force behind recruiting goals. If you know what students want, the next step is to give it to them, and that's more possible than ever thanks to the limitless potential of online technology.

Take another look at that student of the future. If you haven't guessed by now, she's the one who will likely make or break your recruiting efforts. She's in control now, of her future and yours, and she doesn't care about what's been done in the past.

For this to work, college administrators are going to have to face some unpleasant realities. We have a hidebound college culture that can't help but resist change—or at least too much of it. But we also have the tools and technology we need to get the attention of students and their families and the ability to use those tools to get the right kids into the right schools—that is, those "perfect fits" that lead to the win-win scenarios that both colleges and kids want.

Since our communications tools are changing and ever-dynamic, so must be our approach to college admissions recruiting—to create dialogue and to establish a platform for college admissions that will help us right ourselves (we've got some practical suggestions and examples throughout the book) and give us momentum heading into the second decade of the twenty-first century.

Let's keep that momentum going. In the next chapter, we'll take a look at how TargetX began its journey to solving the problems that still plague many colleges and universities. It's a familiar story of how combining business basics with innovation can lead to success—and a way to help the college admissions culture break away from the past.

Chapter 1: The Problem

Rank from 1 to 7 the enrollment management challenges your institution faces.

___ cost of attendance   ___ quality of students

___ lack of leadership   ___ resistance to change

___ loss of funding sources   ___ embracing technology

___ student retention

How does your institution attempt to manage these challenges? What's the culture like when facing adversity?

❑ Leadership takes over and empowers change.

❑ We're able to bring about change, but it's slow and has to come from the ground up.

❑ We form committees, but little seems to get accomplished.

❑ Our institution will continue to do things the same way.

List your "have-to" activities (those you do every year as a rule but don't quite know why).

_____

_____

_____

What recruiting activities are you *not* going to do next year that you have done for the past five years?

_____

_____

_____

2

The Change

We ourselves must be the change we want to see in the world.
—Mahatma Gandhi

It seems that over the past one to two decades, colleges have lived in the world of "if we build it, they will come."

Over this period of time, demographics and easy access to funding for families have converged to provide colleges a well-lit path to profitability and perhaps a false sense of comfort. Tuition has continued to outpace the consumer price index and yet relatively few colleges have had to close their doors because of a lack of demand. The number of high school graduates going on to college has continued to increase and colleges have met consumers' materialistic needs by building fancy residence halls, fitness centers, and technology infrastructure. In addition, funding for college, primarily via student loans, has been abundant and widely accessible.

But that was then and this is now. Today we have reached a tipping point—the point where what seemed to make sense before suddenly doesn't, and not seeing it and adjusting to it threatens our survival. And yet many of us saw this coming. As in the 1990s when the technology boom led to overinflated stock prices of companies that didn't have a business model to support them, the education bubble may be about to burst. We'll discuss this further in other chapters, but suffice it to say I'm not the only one wondering what's next.

Colleges need to learn how to do one thing right now, more than anything: manage and embrace change. While it's easy to pay lip service to change, actually implementing it is another matter.

I say so not just from a thorough review of the past and current collegiate management culture but also from personal experience. Working as an academic recruiter

Instituting Change in College Admissions

As humans, we tend to be change averse—and no more so than in the higher education industry. You've heard the definition of insanity—constantly doing the same thing over, and over expecting a different result.

Genuine progress requires three big changes, and we'll detail those changes later in the book. Success in admissions recruiting requires the following:

- a change in campus culture: "it takes a campus to recruit a student"

- a focus on authenticity: an acceptance of who you are (and who you are not)

- a forward-thinking attitude versus "we've always done it this way"

first at my alma mater and then as a director at a midsize regional university, I found attempts to innovate a tired, "we've always done it this way" system was like beating my head against the wall. Leadership didn't see the value in new technology—it kept adding programs because competitors had them. Plus, we didn't get the resources we needed to do our job and college admissions staffers were some of the most underpaid people on campus.

But with each new idea and each investment into the principles I felt would work, I eventually laid the groundwork for TargetX, the company that would make "overthrowing dead culture" a mantra to live by for college admissions.

But as I said, change isn't easy. The first step is having a plan. As Winston Churchill once said, there is nothing wrong with change, if it is in the right direction. However, this assumes that leadership and others see the need for change. I felt I could be more successful in facilitating change with many universities than while working at one.

For more than a decade, we've worked hard to develop a personal attitude and philosophy to help colleges overcome the old ways of thinking—ways that were holding college recruiters in the technological dark ages. At the root of our thinking was a belief in authenticity—the idea that, when you boil everything down, what consumers really want to know is that you're being true to yourself.

Part of the need to be authentic is that the marketplace demands it these days. In the 1980s, when the baby boomer generation dried up and we didn't have enough people in our dormitory rooms, colleges embraced marketing. Only a few years earlier the College Board launched the student search service, so we at least had a platform to begin fostering change—a place to buy names of prospective students.

Before that, colleges really didn't do "marketing" (in fact not until the 1990s did we even feel comfortable using that word). Back in the 1980s and even before that you pretty much had a catalog, a simple application form and a letter of acceptance or denial—and that was it.

But demographics altered, at least temporarily, the college admissions landscape. All of a sudden we had to get aggressive about marketing because most schools are tuition driven and in the mid-1980s there was a dearth of high school graduates. The proverbial viewbook and admissions video were born, recruiters hit the road for weeks at a time going to high schools and attending college fairs, telemarketing was used, and admissions processes were expanded upon.

Marketing concepts began to solidify in collegiate admissions departments in the 1990s. Companies started talking about branding. "What's your brand?" and "Everyone's got to have a brand" were the buzzwords of the day. I remember it well. You would talk to a new university president back then and, invariably, he or she would expound on the school's branding initiative and tout the new "tagline" developed by an expensive creative marketing firm.

But, as I said earlier, that was then and this is now. Branding was an interesting concept, but in college admissions there is theory and there is execution. Branding fit the bill for the former, but not for the latter. Brand efforts ended up being more who the college wanted to be seen as, not what was seen as reality by their audience.

Today, we increasingly know what works. We believe that now you're going to be hearing more and more about the term "authenticity." But in the insulated world of many in higher education administration, the idea of authenticity becomes lost among the more mainstream marketing approaches governing recruiting. Most schools are more interested in pushing a brand made physical by a glossy, idealized version of the truth. Yet, ironically, most have "Lux" or "Veritas" in their motto or on their seal.

As Jeff Kallay, vice president of consulting at TargetX and self-anointed "Apostle of Authenticity," explains, "Most marketing and advertising render inauthenticity. It's a phoniness-generating machine. College websites, viewbooks—the photography is completely phony." You know those shots—the backpack-toting, awkwardly assembled, very attractive (and very diverse) group of smiling students, posing in front of the most "collegiate" building on campus. They attempt to show an environment that just doesn't exist.

> Search Youtube.com for "honest college ad"—a television commercial for the fictitious "Quendelton State University." It explains inauthenticity in a very funny way ending with, "If we were a good university, we wouldn't have a commercial." *Ouch!*

But here is the reality. Jeff tours five to seven campuses a month and talks to many students, asking them, "Why did you choose this school?" Most of them tell Jeff, "I visited and it felt right." That's it, but the answer is a powerful one. In today's hyper-capitalistic consumption society brands are mirrors. A lot of schools are holding up mirrors that are dirty and foggy and are not reflective of the true nature of the school.

Consequently, despite all the effort schools put into their slick, focus-group-like marketing, the fact remains that a student's thought process when choosing a college is based more on feeling than logic. Rather than point to statistics or testimony or reputation, most students choose their college because it feels like "the right-fit."

And yet if the college isn't going to be true to itself in its marketing and recruiting efforts, its retention rate will surely display its mistakes. There are two main reasons why 60 percent of students attend more than one college before graduating (U.S. Department of Education, 2006) and 53 percent take up to six years to complete their degree (U.S. Department of Education, 2009): they cannot afford it or they wanted something else.

The second reason bothers me because it is avoidable. If the college is authentic in its promotion and gives students the full opportunity to experience what is real before they make the decision to enroll, they are more likely to persist through to graduation at that institution. But instead, colleges continue to try to control a barely honest depiction of their school at the expense of the student (and eventually the college).

Getting Real: Staging an Experience

Of course the problem with terms and phrases like "authenticity" and "the right-fit" is that they don't lend themselves to images or statistics—the kind of information schools use in their attempt to win over recruits. Yet, students are looking for something unquantifiable and intangible. How can schools give students what they really want?

That question is the crux of the "experience economy"—a concept that is at the foundation of what TargetX is attempting to do in the college recruiting game. Coined by authors B. Joseph Pine II and James H. Gilmore in their 1999 Harvard Business School Press book of the same name, the experience economy is one in which consumers are no longer seeking out goods or services—they want experiences. And what businesses must to do to thrive in this type of economy is give consumers that experience, which can be anything from a pleasant memory to, in the case of colleges and universities, a transformation.

According to Pine and Gilmore, the experience economy has five ways of marketing a product or service. The five themes are based on one of the authors' key points—because of technology, increasing competition, and the increasing expectations of consumers, services today are starting to look like commodities. Pine and Gilmore say that products can be placed on a continuum from undifferentiated (referred to as commodities) to highly differentiated. Just as service markets build on goods markets, which in turn build on commodity markets, so transformation and experience markets build on these newly commoditized services, such as Internet bandwidth and consulting help.

The classification for each stage in the evolution of products is the following:

- A commodity business charges for undifferentiated products.

- A goods business charges for distinctive, tangible things.

- A service business charges for the activities you perform.

- An experience business charges for the feeling customers get by engaging it.

- A transformation business charges for the benefit customers (or "guests") receive by spending time there.

Higher education is ultimately selling a transformative experience. Students view college as not only a means to secure a good career, but a chance to grow and evolve as a human being. Being away from family, meeting new friends, going to parties—the transformation experience is already formed in the student's mind before he even steps foot on a real campus.

In the experience economy, the idea of providing that experience and a college's need to be authentic go hand in hand. As Pine and Gilmore point out in their other book, *Authenticity*, people are looking for something deeper from companies these days. Consumers are more sophisticated; the ways in which they interact with companies are more varied and have fewer controls in place. As mentioned before, consumers—especially teenagers—are adept in the art of sniffing out corporate marketing and other perceived inauthentic modes of communication. Brochures with photos of perfectly groomed, neatly posed students? Statistics reaped from some faceless polling organization? Those are inauthentic, and it's why they don't work that well anymore in college recruiting.

Colleges are also selling a premium-priced service. Think Starbucks. It's still coffee at the heart of it, but they are selling the experience and customization. Sound familiar? And they get away with selling it at a premium price (if you had asked me ten years ago whether I would spend $3.50 on a cup of coffee some day, I'd think you were off your rocker!). But instead of embracing the experience and justifying the premium price accordingly, we discount our price, devaluing the benefit derived from attending our institution.

The Experience Economy

In *The Experience Economy*, Pine and Gilmore describe the experience economy as the one following the agrarian, the industrial, and the most recent service economy.

Businesses must orchestrate memorable events for their customers, they argue, and that memory itself becomes the product—the "experience." More advanced experience businesses can begin charging for the value of the "transformation" that an experience offers, for example as education offerings might do if they were able to participate in the value that is created by the educated individual. This, they argue, is a natural progression in the value added by the business over and above its inputs.

Although the concept of the experience economy was born in the business field, it has crossed frontiers to tourism, architecture, nursing, urban planning and other fields. The experience economy is also considered a main underpinning for customer experience management—an important theme for twenty-first century colleges and universities.

The Business of Education

So, what does TargetX do to help colleges be themselves online, in print, and in person? Well, let's put aside, just for a moment, everything that's been discussed so far. Forget about authenticity and put the Internet out of your mind. What TargetX really does to change recruiting is abide by a principle that, while seemingly obvious, often gets overlooked in the high-minded, noble world of higher education. And that principle is that colleges are first and foremost a business, and recruiting is a sales effort.

Colleges are businesses and students (and their parents) are their customers. Colleges provide a product or service, they take money in return for that product or service, they have expenses and pay employees, and they may or may not make a profit at the end of the day. That's a business. Once we accept that, we will start to rethink a few things including our vision, who we hire, what resources we provide, and where we invest.

In the multitude of seminars and presentations I give, I invariably point out that the main problem inherent in the old college recruiting model is that we forget that, as admissions professionals, we are really salespeople.

Now before you get angry and slam down this book, let's make sure we're not think-ing about the traditional type of salesperson. The first thing most people envision when they think of a salesperson is the one found on a used car lot who is stereotyped as dishonest, manipulative and heartless. That is not a good salesperson.

A good salesperson is one who has something to provide that he or she believes in and is looking for people who are looking for that something. It's matching a product or service to the right customer. Sounds a lot like how I was trained as an admissions counselor almost twenty years ago.

If you accept the premise that admissions professionals are actually sales people, you may start to make some different decisions. Is it really in your best interest to hire a recent graduate who has no experience selling anything? Do you think it would be a better idea to provide your admissions staff regular professional sales training programs? What technology choices would you make? Would you give them the tools (computer, cell phone, customer relationship management, etc.) they need to get the job done?

What TargetX recognizes—and what is at the heart of its approach to recruiting—is that a school needs to balance the need for authenticity with the real business skills it takes to be successful. A school needs to find the right people for the job, and then needs to give them the right training to get the job done. This has been the human resources philosophy of TargetX from day one. Hire the best people you can afford, pay them well, give them what they need, and get out of their way.

Stories Not Stats, People Not Programs

So, colleges need to be authentic, and they need to develop a keen business mind-set. Clearly, the old ways of trying to reach out to students are seen as out of touch by today's college-bound population.

So there's that *change* issue again. How to adapt? How to revolutionize? How to overcome decades of atrophied admissions strategies?

It's all too easy to simply say "go online" because that's just a medium. The message is as important and is common to online, print, and in-person activities.

Many years ago I heard Michael Sexton, the director of admissions at Lewis and Clark College, say, "Stories not stats. People not programs." It was my professional "ah ha!" moment. Look at most college websites or viewbooks and what you'll find is a bunch of statistics about the school ("founded in 1856, we have over 5,000 students and a student-to-faculty ratio of ... blah blah blah") and a list of programs and activi-ties—most of which you could slap another college's logo on and call it a day.

Up until the advent of the Internet, much of what college recruiting had been about was what we call "talk-at" marketing—where the medium, the message and the timing are all controlled by the admissions office when in fact today's young generation grew up experiencing interactive (or *talk with*) media, particularly online.

The most authentic thing about a college is the people who go there and the stories they can share. Embrace stories—online, in print, and in person.

After all, authenticity thrives on the Internet. It's the breeding ground for the revolutionary, warts-and-all social media giants like MySpace, Facebook, and Twitter. There's no branding or marketing involved—users create the content, usually with no larger audience in mind than their friends. Social media is the natural response from a generation that had grown cynical of the transparent, inauthentic ways mega corporations have tried to curry their favor. And colleges are in the perfect position to harness it.

When we started TargetX in 1998, we were looking for a way to reach students online. They weren't coming out to college and graduate fairs like they used to—they were going online and getting the information they needed. And it wasn't always accurate and sometimes simply not what we wanted out there. But it was as real as it could get and we couldn't hide the warts anymore. And yet still some colleges believe they control the message, eschewing social networks, blogs, and instant messaging, fearing something bad might be said.

And by the way, the only step of the recruiting funnel a college controls is if they decide to accept or reject the student's application. That's it. The student controls every other stage of the process (if they inquire, apply, deposit, enroll, persist), as well as what they decide to read and write online about you.

Back then, of course, there was no Facebook or MySpace and the Internet was still in its infancy as far as being a mass communication tool. I'm not going to snow you—we did see some promise in technology tools geared toward college admissions; we just needed to figure out how to fit the stodgy, formal world of college recruiting into this exciting new online frontier. We started with email recruiting—what has become commonplace today (spam and all) was new and exciting—which was an easy, inexpensive way to reach a lot of people quickly and measure the results in real time.

In fact, the night we figured that out was the night we scribbled everything down on a cocktail napkin, the night TargetX was born.

Ten Ways to Manage Change

Over the past ten years of trying to figure this stuff out, I've come up with ten key themes in fostering change in college admissions and higher education leadership.

1. **Differentiate or Die** Each college must dig deep inside and determine who they are and, perhaps more important, who they are not. This takes visionary leaders who must make more strategic decisions where the answer is "no" than they may be comfortable with. Passing on perceived good opportunities in favor of other, more authentic ones is sound strategy. It starts at the top and must be fed to the front line to communicate why your institution should be chosen over another. Positioning against your competitors (note I didn't call them "peer institutions") takes skill and experience. But it also takes a visionary to get the ball rolling.

2. **Do What You Do Best (and Outsource the Rest)** Colleges are in business to educate. They are not in business to provide food services, run a bookstore, manage administrative technology, or oversee housing, just to name a few. Find the areas where someone else has figured out a more cost-effective way to provide them and get them off your plate. Then focus on what you do best. You'll thank yourself in the morning.

3. **Get Everyone Onboard (or Get Them Off)** Look first at your management team. Are they the right players? Are they in the right position? Who are you looking out for as future leaders and who saps you of your energy because they "just don't get it"? You need the right players on your team, and not always those who agree with you. Our philosophy is *hire people smarter than us*. Do you? Does your campus entirely embrace recruiting? Read the story about Elon University in George Keller's *Transforming a College*.

4. **Share Information (Especially Financials)** Information is power. Empower your people. Give them the information they need to make sound decisions. Sometimes this is financial: many times this is your vision as a department or institutional leader. Don't hold anything back (except for compensation data). The more they know, the more they can help (if you follow the previous tip).

5. **Question Everything** Get out of your office, eat lunch with your students, ask them questions—they are the only ones who can tell you what it is like to be a "customer" of your college or university. Ask your prospective students at each stage of the funnel, "Are you still interested in us?" "Is there something that might not make us a good fit?" "What do you need me to do to make this happen?"

6. **Watch Your Language** Start using words like *business, sales, customers, return on investment.* People may at first look at you funny, but they'll catch on. It wasn't too long ago the word *marketing* bothered people in higher education, but we got over it and ended up embracing it.

7. **Read Different Stuff** It's fine to read the *Chronicle of Higher Education, Campus Technology, Academic Impressions,* and other industry-based publications; you are not the only ones marketing to this audience. There are others with more resources from which you can learn. Get a subscription to the magazine *Fast Company*. Pick up a copy of *Advertising Age* and subscribe to the daily email newsletter. The same goes for professional development. Instead of attending an industry event, go to All Things Digital or Think About or YPulse, to name a few.

8. **Avoid Paralysis through Leadership** Higher education administration was founded on the idea of *shared governance,* meaning basically all have a place at the table. And while the "it takes a community" approach makes for a unique and special environment, it can't paralyze us from decision-making. A committee cannot be made accountable—only individuals can be. That doesn't take away from involving others in the information-gathering process. But colleges today, more than ever, need clear vision and decisive leadership. Hire great people, give them the resources they need, get out of their way, and hold them accountable for their actions or inactions.

9. **Embrace Urgency** Now is not the time to have a group of team members who are complacent or have what John Kotter termed "false urgency" in his book *A Sense of Urgency* (being always busy but not really getting anything significant accomplished). If you find yourself hiring lots of consultants, setting deadlines but always missing them, or having a hard time scheduling meetings, you have an organizational problem embracing urgency. Today's business requires a continual sense of urgency that is not only fast-paced but, more important, smart and focused.

10. **Take the Chairs Away** Again, committees can't be held accountable, only individuals can be. And colleges are riddled with committees and standing meetings with little accountability or goals taking place in comfy conference rooms, allowing attendees to get comfortable for hours at a time. A president at a Northeast college planted the idea in my mind many years ago that conference rooms shouldn't have chairs. People have to meet, but they don't always have to sit down to get something accomplished. Take away the chairs and the standing committees. Instead, embrace task forces that have a clear end and a decision-maker running them.

Chapter 2: The Change

What aspect of your college or university could be more effectively told as a personal story?

_____

_____

_____

_____

_____

What is the most "inauthentic" aspect of your college's marketing efforts?

_____

_____

_____

_____

Do any of these describe the culture at your college or university?

❑ Regularly hire external consultants

❑ Difficulty scheduling meetings on important issues

❑ Have a committee that is charged with creating other committees

❑ Frequently missing deadlines on critical action steps

❑ Discussions focused inward instead of based on market forces

❑ Failures of the past stop or stall new initiatives

3

The Customer

Stop flirting with me. Stop trying so hard. Stop killing trees.
Answer me. Communicate with me.
—Responses from high school students to a TargetX/The
Southern Association for College Admission Counseling survey about
their perceptions on how colleges communicate with them

I don't think it's a secret that today's high school students—Millennials—are revolutionizing the way colleges communicate with prospective students.

It's an uprising that schools will pay dearly to ignore. Colleges that pay lip service to the revolution risk losing more students to colleges that do a better job of communicating with students, especially in the long-neglected area of storytelling.

The current crop of college-bound students, part of the generation born after 1981, are different from their predecessors in the way they respond to information. These teenagers are much more interactive. They want to converse with colleges, not be marketed to. They want to be able to ask questions and comment on what they see and hear. They demand the unvarnished truth and are extremely resistant to hype and advertising speak.

I call this new environment Recruiting 2.0. Under the new rules of college recruiting, you can no longer talk-at students through publications, direct mail, static websites, and generic email broadcasts. Millennials don't want any part of that. What they really want is for college admissions departments to open a dialogue with them.

It sounds trite, but that dialogue has to be real; it has to be authentic. Colleges can't rely on slick marketing copy to tell the story of their school. They have to tell stories. Further, they need to plug their "authentic" resources into the conversation by letting their current students and faculty and alumni explain what differentiates their school from other colleges—and in their own words. Teens find that much more believable and authentic.

It really is time for a change. The Recruiting 2.0 concept reflects my belief that colleges have been marketing the same way since they realized thirty years ago that they had to compete for students by producing slick brochures and direct mail campaigns.

Even when colleges started recruiting online in the late 1990s, they simply communicated electronically the way they were communicating with ink and paper. Now students are forcing a revolution in the way colleges recruit. Version 1.0 won't work with this group, so it's time for a new phase that is more interactive, more candid, less controlled. It's finally time for an upgrade.

Upgrading to Recruiting 2.0

An upgrade is exactly what today's high school students need. And they're demanding it.

That's what Matthew Robson has in mind.

Robson was a fifteen-year-old intern for Morgan Stanley, where he wrote a mind-blowing report for the investment banking giant on how he and his teenage friends consume media.

It's a lesson that we in the college admissions field should take to heart. The report is a real eye-opener on what high school kids want from the media and, by extension, what kids want from colleges using media formats like the web and cell phones in reaching out to attractive collegiate candidates.

I won't cite the report chapter and verse, but parts of it are highly instructional. In his paper, Robson says the following:

On Newspapers "No teenager that I know of regularly reads a newspaper, as most do not have the time and cannot be bothered to read pages and pages of text while they could watch the news summarized on the Internet or on TV. The only newspapers that are read are tabloids and free sheets (Metro, London Late) mainly because of cost; teenagers are very reluctant to pay for a newspaper (hence the popularity of free sheets such as the Metro)."

On the Internet "Every teenager has some access to the Internet, be it at school or home. Home use is mainly used for fun (such as social networking) whilst school (or library) use is for work. Most teenagers are heavily active on a combination of social networking sites. Facebook is the most common, with nearly everyone with an Internet connection registered and visiting >4 times a week. Facebook is popular as one can interact with friends on a wide scale."

On Twitter "On the other hand, teenagers do not use Twitter. Most have signed up to the service, but then just leave it as they realize that they are not going to update it (mostly because texting twitter uses up credit, and they would rather text friends with that credit). In addition, they realize that no one is viewing their profile, so their 'tweets' are pointless. Outside of social networking, the Internet is used primarily as a source of information for a variety of topics."

On Viral/Outdoor Marketing "Most teenagers enjoy and support viral marketing, as often it creates humorous and interesting content. Teenagers see adverts on websites (pop ups, banner ads) as extremely annoying and pointless, as they have never paid any attention to them and they are portrayed in such a negative light that no one follows them."

On Mobile Phones "Ninety-nine percent of teenagers have a mobile phone and most are quite capable phones. Usually, teenagers only use their phone for texting, calling. Features such as video messaging or video calling are not used—because they are expensive (you can get four regular texts for the price of one video message)."

On Instant Messaging "Services such as instant messaging are used, but not by everyone. It usually depends whether the phone is WiFi compatible, because otherwise it is very expensive to get Internet off the phone network. As most teenagers' phones have Bluetooth support, and Bluetooth is free, they use this feature often."

Straight from the Source

Although Robson encapsulates what I hear from a lot of teenagers, and does it very impressively, he's hardly alone. What his generation of high school students wants from media platforms echoes what it wants when dealing with college recruiters.

Case in point: I recently sat in a podcast with a group of very bright, very ambitious high school students, where a key topic was what the kids wanted from the colleges they chose to attend.

The show was hosted by a high school senior, Abby Laporte. Called "Abby's Road" her show was a live webcast and podcast chronicling Abby's search for the right college and her life as a high school senior. "Abby's Road" is intended to be a weekly documentary about her journey from high school to college and life as a high school senior—starting with her college search and continuing through her senior year and into enrollment at college.

It was a lively, vibrant discussion. By and large, high school students are realistic—they know that colleges have their hands full recruiting and then educating thousands of college students each year.

But there are some expectations where the high school students I spoke to wouldn't give an inch. For example, they want the ability to interact with colleges online through websites, email, text messaging, online chats, or blogs, or through social networking sites like Facebook.

One trend I do see developing—and one that I support wholeheartedly—is that high school students are encouraged by counselors to build a relationship with someone at the college. That's what students want—someone with whom they can develop a relationship throughout the recruitment process. They want a familiar name on an email address, an IM screen name, or phone number.

Even so, too many colleges just don't dot the "i"s on this one. I know of one admissions counselor who used the following automated voicemail message when he was out of town: "I'll be away from the office for two weeks, so leave a message." So if potential students or parents wanted to reach the counselor, they had to email or call and wait for him to return to the office. Are you kidding me? The takeaway for students and families is a horrible one: the counselor doesn't have time to recruit because he's too busy recruiting.

There's another young person, wise beyond his years, who has some great thoughts on what the younger generation wants from the older one. His name is Josh Shipp, and he's a twenty-something phenomenon. Abandoned and abused as a child, he overcame those obstacles to become a successful motivational speaker while still in his teens. He has developed a special affinity with the Millennial generation, who see him as part older brother and part Dear Abby.

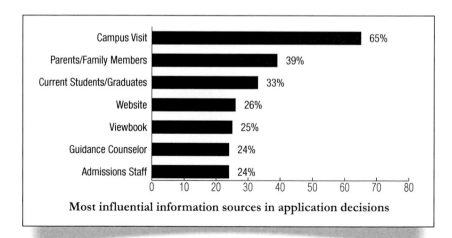

Most influential information sources in application decisions

Shipp is now a go-to source on Millennials for everyone from TV producers to product-peddling corporations. In a recent interview with writer Kimberly Smith of MarketingProfs, Shipp lays down the law on what kids expect from businesses looking to get their attention and, by extension, from college admissions professionals looking to get them to come to their schools.

- **Don't speak down to them** Nobody likes that, but to really connect with this group you need to take it a step further and actually talk above their age levels. If they're fifteen, think of them as twenty-five. They don't get a lot of that, so when people do treat them as if they're older, there's usually a good response.

- **Offer up a good story** Teens don't relate to companies or brands; they relate to stories. This penchant stems partly from their desire to be entertained but also from a need to identify with and understand where an organization is coming from. Providing Millennials with an intriguing, meaningful, and authentic story that they can associate with and recount to their friends is one key to sparking a connection.

- **Don't overestimate their differences** This generation may have characteristics different from those of other groups, but at the end of the day these basic truths still hold true: They seek love, friendship, acceptance, and respect. They want to look good, feel cool, and have fun socializing with friends. If you can give them that, and do it well, they will respond.

This is exactly why we go out of our way to talk with high school students and search out the expertise of younger Americans who have a lot to say about what their generation wants from the college experience.

College presidents should be doing the exact same thing.

Knowing What Students Want

Knowing what students like Abby Laporte and Matthew Robson want—and in what mediums they prefer to communicate their messages—is at the heart and soul of this new generation of the college admissions market.

The stakes are way too high not to understand what students really want from colleges.

Put it this way. Consider the case of a northeastern college that lost 30 percent of its endowment in the economic collapse of the last few years. That's bad news for the college, which gets a third of its operating budget from its endowment. Now the college's president is publicly fretting about how the school is weathering the downturn, implementing layoffs, early retirement packages, cuts in services, and even changes

Hiring Customer-Conscious Admissions Representatives

Giving students and their families what they want is simply good customer service. I encourage college presidents to hire college admissions staffers who have experience as a sales or customer service representative. Today's college admissions representatives should have knowledge and training in the sales and customer service fields. Admissions representatives do a lot of promoting, advertising, communicating, and networking with the general public, so having a background in sales/customer service is very important.

to breakfast menus for undergraduates. The college president also knows that any further reductions in the endowment distribution next year will mean more cuts.

The college in question? Prestigious Harvard University.

You know if Harvard's president is publicly worried about how the economy is messing with the school's financial picture, then every other college is worried, too.

Hence, the ever-increasing need to thoroughly understand what students want— think customer service for the collegiate admissions set.

I understand that it's not easy for colleges to think like a *real* business and think of students as *customers*. Other industries already understand that the first step for any business is to understand what their consumer base is looking for. Starting a clothing boutique? You'd better know what the latest fashions are. The same principle is true for colleges. You've got to know your students.

To give you an example, I was recently sent an email by the director of admissions at Baldwin-Wallace College in Ohio. My colleagues had just conducted a tour guide training session there, and she wanted to let me know what one recruit had to say about a recent campus tour.

As you'll learn later in this book, campus tours can be either great or complete bombs, so we were prepared for anything. But as it turned out, this kid loved his tour. The reason why? His tour guide, Jarvis. This student told the director of admissions all about how Jarvis was honest, how Jarvis was real and personal. Jarvis never walked backward. You can probably see where I'm going with this: Jarvis was being authentic.

Instead of leading a company line, one-size-fits-all tour, Jarvis gave the student "real" college advice, the email said. There was no hard sell being pitched, at least from the student's point of view; Jarvis had even implied that Baldwin-Wallace might not be the best fit for him, and that was okay. The point is that Jarvis—and by extension Baldwin-Wallace College—wasn't pretending to be anything other than who he was. Today's students respond to that kind of authenticity; it's what they look for in a college, even if they can't always express it to your admissions staff.

I think there's a lot colleges can learn from Jarvis. Students aren't just looking for a great education from their future college; they're also after that memorable, *just feels right* experience, which often comes down to the little things, as my email example shows.

Getting into a Student's Head

As a groundbreaking study from the academic research group Education Conservancy attests, data do exist that pretty much cement what students want from the college admissions experience—and what they don't want.

Key findings from the organization's report titled "College Admissions: What Are Students Learning?" crystallize the customer-service mind-set that students are demonstrating in their college search practices.

Like a customer at a car dealership who wants certain features in his new set of wheels or a restaurant patron who wants her Cobb salad made a certain way, students are increasingly showing, loudly and clearly, that they have their preferences and expectations, too. This is mass customization epitomized by Starbucks.

For example, high school students searching for the right college strongly dislike disingenuous college recruiting. They don't want to read plain-Jane generic marketing materials. They're overwhelmed, and thus vastly annoyed, by college fairs, and they believe that information sessions are unappealing and too much like sales pitches.

Students also strongly disapprove of being urged to apply to a university even when they have no chance of admission. They feel that often schools are simply trying to serve themselves by courting students' money (application fees) and applications (only to reject them).

Job One: Managing Expectations

That said, there are some things students definitely want. For example, high school students who consider themselves "specialists," that is, on their way to an engineering, journalism, or law degree, want that specialty (or uniqueness) recognized by colleges. Consequently, schools must work to specifically identify what kind of student body they want and understand what kind of experiences these kids will be looking for. And from a general standpoint, what we do know about college recruits is that

The Cost of Not Giving Students What They Want

A recent report from the National Research Center for College and University Admissions (NRCCUA) concludes that colleges and universities are turning off potential students because their websites don't meet student expectations.

"Today's technically savvy generation of students has extremely high expectations when it comes to the amount and type of admissions information they find on university websites," said Don Munce, president of NRCCUA. "Meeting these expectations with quality, up-to-date websites will help students better navigate the admissions process and ensure that colleges and universities are attracting students in the Internet generation."

In the study of over 3,000 college and university websites, only 140 institutions received a grade of A, 713 received a B, 1,369 received a C, 635 a D, and 230 an F. No sites scored in the 90s or 80s on the index's 100-point scale; only 16 scored in the 70s, and nearly one-third earned scores in the 50s or 60s. Scores for the top 10 schools ranged from 71 to 74 on the 100-point scale, a significant decrease from last year's top scores of 78 to 82.

Students said they were less likely to attend a school whose websites didn't meet their needs, the organization says.

they know the admissions game pretty well even before they start filling out applications. Most of them know the high stakes; they know who the top players are and what it takes to impress them. By the time they're done, they may know it too well. In fact, the survey by the Education Conservancy found that many students interviewed felt worn down by the process and had become cynical of college admissions and even education in general.

That's an important theme—and one that is underplayed by colleges but very much on the minds of the high school students I talked to on Abby's podcast. Thus, an important point to remember about recruiting is that you're dealing, for the most part, with a very emotional and vulnerable kind of client. These kids are putting their hearts and souls on the line to get into the college they've imagined for themselves. Some know right from the beginning where they think they belong; others are waiting to find that perfect fit. Many students will experience disappointment—even heartbreak—before they find their eventual college.

Consequently, it's no surprise that students feel pressure—pressure to take certain tests and advanced classes, to join certain clubs, and to attain certain ranks, all to impress admissions committees. They also feel insignificant, in the sense that they believe factors beyond their control contribute heavily to schools' enrollment decisions—factors such as a student's wealth and connections, for instance. Students also feel they aren't getting straight information from schools, which only further complicates their feelings about themselves and what they feel they should be or how they should appear to college admissions boards.

Toss the parents into that mix and you may have something combustible—and something you may not be able to control. By our own experiences, we know that parents are usually just as stressed and anxious as their student, for different reasons. They want to make sure their son or daughter will get the best education available. But they also have concerns about finances, living situations, and other more practical matters. In past years, parents often would be as emotionally invested in their child's college choice as the student him- or herself. Now? Parents are a little more discerning, and less apt to go for the big-name school and the budget-busting costs that go with it.

So what does this mean for colleges? Well, for one thing, admissions staff must cut through this wall of insecurities and establish a foundation of trust and familiarity. But it also means that students as well as their parents are both constantly looking for different kinds of reassurances during the admissions process. Students want to know where they stand with a college and how they will fit into its culture. Parents want to know that the school and its representatives know what they're doing. In the days of sky-high tuitions and relentless college marketing, families are more cynical and more likely to look for schools that run the best businesses.

Other conclusions from the Education Conservancy Study:

- Students feel pressured to do things for the sole purpose of gaining admission, such as participating in extracurricular activities, taking multiple AP or IB courses, or engaging in various forms of SAT preparation. Students feel it is impossible to be everything colleges would like them to be.

- Students receive conflicting messages from colleges. Colleges say they want well-rounded students, which is discouraging for many students with concentrated passions or unique qualities. Colleges also seem to expect students to have decided on their majors and what their life goals are.

- Colleges say they are unique, but their marketing materials (online and print) make them all sound the same to many students.

- Students believe that colleges cannot, and do not, judge applicants in a fair and objective way.

- Students agree that too much emphasis is placed on attending a prestigious college but admit that the prestige of a college does matter to them. They believe if they go to a better college they will get a better job and have more success in life.

- Although students believe that the advantages of legacy connections are *just part of life*, they feel that students should not be defined by what their parents have done but by what they themselves have done.

- Private school students recognized the advantage they have over students at public schools because of their wealthier family backgrounds, legacies at some institutions, and having access to more resources, like SAT preparation.

- Private school students were less critical of dishonesty and cheating in the application process than were public school students, believing that it is just part of the game.

- Students wanted to know the importance of essay question responses, SAT scores, and AP classes, and if they were really supposed to decide on a major and know their goals for their future before finishing high school.

- Students would like to have honest, straightforward information about application criteria from admissions personnel. Students were unsure of what colleges are really looking for and felt that colleges should be more up-front.

- Students experienced extreme stress due to the college application process. Worrying, emotional instability, sleeping problems, eating problems, and a variety of physical symptoms due to those stressors were commonly reported.

From a marketing perspective, the survey shows that students take a dim view of the current state of the college admissions marketing process. Current college marketing programs are, as the Education Conservancy report states, "viewed by students as self-serving, deceptive, and often inconsistent with how students think colleges should act."

In addition, widespread marketing messages that "we are the best and the best for you" appear implausible to students. Consequently, the report concludes, marketing activity and rhetoric employed by colleges contribute to healthy skepticism, but also to cynicism, distrust, and unethical behavior.

The college admissions process is not viewed as fair by many students. They see the evidence of class and racial privilege, as well as the role of connections, special interests, and talent. They see a lack of connection between the values of hard work and dedication and the particular ways in which admissions decisions are made (i.e., what types of characteristics are rewarded). A most striking area of concern is the unjustified importance of the SAT. The SAT appears to contribute to both cynicism about institutions and acceptance of some types of cheating, which one student called, "equal opportunity cheating." Students believe the SAT plays a significant role in college admissions that is patently unfair. They do not understand how four hours of testing, which they believe can be improved by coaching that focuses on strategy and gamesmanship, can be anywhere near as appropriate to assessing potential for success in college and later in life as four years of education and the effort it requires to succeed in high school.

What Abby Wants

As the high school kids in Abby's podcast told me, students know that they're being judged at every turn.

What's more, they're used to high-up authority figures who control every aspect of their education—it's what most of them saw in high school. What they're looking for at college is a chance to be themselves, to find new and productive outlets for their abilities and personal quirks. They don't want to be marketed to, or talked down to, or treated as if they're yet another cog on the assembly line just waiting to be inserted into a school's prearranged student body.

Be Authentic

I hear this all the time. Students are especially interested in hearing real voices talk about real college experiences because it's one of the few opportunities they have to learn about what they consider the "real" college experience, the one not mentioned in admissions publications and campus tours.

Ultimately, when you look at each of the factors in the admissions equation, you have the students who are looking for that emotional, personal experience, and their parents, who are probably searching for a cost-effective, organized operation. These two viewpoints are neither mutually exclusive nor all that different from each other; in fact, they complement each other. They're both looking for a college that will be authentic.

Sometimes being authentic means having to give up a little control. You need to be able to tell students and their parents the truth about what your college will offer. But you also can do this in a way that makes what you're offering seem unique. Hendrix College knows that it isn't a school for everybody, but it maximizes the things it's honestly good at and highlights them. That's what being authentic is all about. You can be true to yourself and hope that people will respond to it.

To approach this point another way, people have a very difficult time differentiating between levels of quality in the marketplace. This is especially true in higher education, where you have the top schools and then all the rest. What makes an expensive liberal arts school a better education experience than a highly ranked state college? You can look at statistics to a point, but most families won't have the time or inclination to spend that much time researching the merits of one school's science department versus a dozen others.

But families will always be able to recognize authenticity because authenticity stands on its own; you don't need to compare it to anything. The student in the email I mentioned earlier in the chapter didn't look at Jarvis the tour guide in terms of metrics; he wasn't the third best tour guide or the best tour guide at a liberal arts school in Ohio. He was just a great guide and a person that a student could identify with.

In the next chapter, I'm going to delve deeper into this relationship between colleges and families. I'll explore the importance of storytelling, the dynamics of the "elevator pitch," and how colleges can build an effective recruiting platform that will resonate with both students and parents. It's the first step to establishing an authentic experience in the college admissions process.

Chapter 3: The Customer

Describe the "best-fit" students for your institution:

_____

_____

_____

_____

Ask a current student (preferably a first-year student) to grade your college's website on how it meets the needs of prospective students and families (take notes).

Notes: _____

_____

_____

_____

Grade: _____

Review with the same student how you go about recruiting future students.

What should you stop doing? _____

_____

_____

What should you start doing? _____

_____

_____

The Message

*Be who you are and say what you feel because those who mind don't matter
and those who matter don't mind.*
—Dr. Seuss

Earlier, we mentioned the phrase "Stories not stats. People not programs." These are key themes that college administrators need to consider before they can genuinely—and effectively—change their admissions culture.

At TargetX, we've given a lot of thought to the issue of messaging. What have we found? That there's no mystery to good storytelling. It's all about looking in the mirror and asking yourself, "Who am I?"

This is a process we like to call *finding your institutional DNA*—and communicating that message to your audience. After all, what influences potential students isn't impressive statistics or how many buildings you've erected on campus but how your story resonates with their lives.

The formula for doing that isn't complicated. High school kids want to know how they'll relate to life on campus; how they'll get along with other students; or how they'll interact with their professors. Students want to see themselves at your school; they want to see themselves trading clips from YouTube with a fellow student or strolling through the campus center; they want to visualize themselves working alongside a teacher in a clinical laboratory.

The best way that students can step from visualization to actualization is by "seeing" your college through stories, that is, shared experiences that lead high school kids to smile, nod their heads, and say to themselves, "Yeah, I can easily see myself here."

It's like the old maxim that the best way to a man's heart is through his stomach. For colleges, the way to a student's heart is through storytelling—the more human, the better.

The Albright College Story

I've talked to hundreds of college administrators and have heard all of their stories. The best ones, and they are out there, are the ones that show—and not tell—students who they are and what life is really like on their campus.

A wonderful example of an institution finding stories through their students' voices can be found in Reading, Pennsylvania, at Albright College. A few years ago, Albright launched a four-color magazine-style publication called *Faces* to replace their traditional viewbook.

In *Faces*, students told stories (accompanied by plenty of professionally shot photos) about classes, friends, dining hall, athletics, jobs, internships, secret spots on campus, and other things about the school. Essentially, *Faces* is a series of publications highlighting individual students and professors who share their personal stories and experiences. Each person's page includes a link to their blog on the college's social network so prospective students and parents can jump online and interact with the individual. In-person events, such as open houses, provide opportunities for visitors to meet some of the "faces" they've read about and corresponded with in the publications and online.

But importantly, students were also encouraged to show their individual personalities, which in turn enriched the personality of the school. Since the profiles included every kind of student, they helped many prospective students picture themselves watching movies in their dorm or taking part in a famous Albright tradition—*ponding* fellow students on their birthday.

Imagine that. Relying on Albright students and professors to describe what makes the college and its people so special, and to tell the stories online, in print, and in person as part of a fully integrated communications campaign.

Full disclosure: We had worked with Albright on the *Faces* campaign, helping them develop a recruiting communications campaign consisting of a series of unique publications, a new college website, online tools favored by college-bound students, and enhanced in-person events for admitted applicants.

What we did, I believe, fits right into the themes I'm bringing to the table in this chapter. The campaign revolved around the theme of *Faces* to focus on the people of Albright and their personal stories instead of the traditional method of promoting programs and statistics.

More on Institutional DNA

In our travels across the country touting the benefits of change as it applies to college admissions and recruiting, we spend a great deal of time talking about a pretty simple concept—knowing who you are.

We know, it seems obvious, and everyone we talk to—we're talking about deans and college presidents here—seems to think they know, in a nutshell, what their school is all about.

But do they really? The evidence we see says it's just not so. In fact, when we actually ask college officials to explain their college in a sentence or less—to give us their "story"—We get a blank look not unlike a salmon lying on a table at the Seattle Fish Market.

This shouldn't be so. Why? Because all of the evidence we've seen demonstrates that a school that knows who they are—and there aren't as many as you'd think—have more success recruiting students.

We could have devoted an entire chapter to managing a college's brand and messages. In fact, many have written their own books on those subjects. But we believe the most critical aspect to marketing communications in today's fast-paced world isn't what colleges write about themselves in their viewbook or on their website. It's how they answer the questions who are you, what makes you special, and why should I care, and do it with brevity.

In other words, your *institutional DNA.*

Albright was astute about its new storytelling program. It knew, for example, that students are starting their college search earlier in high school and are spending 75 percent of their time searching online. They understood that kids are looking for real stories from real people and are turned off by marketing-speak. And, most important, they recognized that students are attending on-campus events in greater numbers than ever before but are looking for authenticity and differentiation.

The success of the campaign isn't in doubt. "I talked recently with a group of students visiting our campus," said Albright's admissions director, Chris Boehm, "and when I asked them why they decided to come and see us, all of them said that one reason was they really felt they connected with the student stories they read in *Faces.* It's very rewarding to see a plan succeed that way."

Storytelling in the Technology Age

A while back, our marketing guru at TargetX, Ray Ulmer, wrote on our iThink blog that marketers tend to obsess over the tools behind social networking's meteoric rise. They wonder, are blogs more effective than Facebook? How easy is Ning to use? Does Twitter appeal to young people?

But what they're forgetting is huge. Ray points to social strategist Gaurav Mishra, who believes that the tools are not as important as the content. And the content that continues to engage people most consistently is a good story.

"I have come to the conclusion that social media is most powerful when it's used for creating, collecting and sharing stories," Mishra wrote. "In fact, I now believe that storytelling is the key to social media marketing success."

Stories are central to the human condition, he says. We love to listen to stories. We're able to learn from stories. And we enjoy sharing stories.

That's a powerful combination, and one that social media can take advantage of—especially our inclination to share. "We share stories to build relationships, build kinship, as individuals and as groups," says Mishra. "Sharing stories comes almost as naturally to us as remembering to breathe."

Colleges are fortunate to have an unlimited number of stories to share—from students, faculty and alumni. By telling these stories, they make it possible for prospective students to relate to your school and see themselves as part of the community.

Social networking is really about conversations, says Mishra, and the most engaging conversations involve the exchange of stories.

Connecting With Millennials

Albright's experience is living proof of what colleges need to recognize: that high-school-age Millennials are revolutionizing the way colleges communicate with prospective students. Make no mistake, storytelling is a huge part of that revolution.

The stories may be instrumental, as they have been for decades, but the means of transporting those stories has changed dramatically in this, the Information Age. How so? Today's Millennials are vastly different from their predecessors in the way they respond to information. They are much more interactive and they want to converse with colleges, not be marketed to. They want to be able to ask questions and comment on what they see and hear. Above all, they demand the unvarnished truth and are extremely resistant to hype and advertising-speak.

Storytelling 101

In a recent survey by Maguire Associates, an educational consulting firm in Concord, Massachusetts which was published by the *Chronicle of Higher Education,* college admissions officials say certain storytelling tools work better than others.

According to the Maguire study, blogs from current college students posted on the colleges websites and online chats have become two of the most popular ways for colleges to recruit applicants, according to the colleges surveyed. "After most prospective students have sorted through the factual information (majors, location, size, etc.) these student-oriented media help with *the* key question: Where do I fit best?" says Tom Weede, vice president of enrollment at Butler University. Cheryl Brown, director of undergraduate admissions at SUNY-Binghamton, thinks applicants turn to student blogs, which appear on the school's website, because "they want the 'real story,' not marketing-generated canned materials." She says, "Today's students believe blogs, IMs, and other true-to-life contacts to be more believable."

How can schools accomplish this interaction so their stories have maximum impact? By finding a new level of truth telling through the technologies that today's teens know and love best, including instant messaging, blogs, podcasts, personalized email, and text messaging.

You can no longer talk-at students through publications, direct mail, static websites, and email broadcasts. You have to open a dialogue with them.

And you can't rely on slick marketing copy to tell the story of your school. You have to let your current students and faculty and alumni explain what differentiates you from other colleges—and in their own words. Teens find that much more believable and authentic.

Besides, students can still find statistical information if they want it—for example, by checking the school's website for more detail or collegeboard.com (or any number of growing websites with such information).

Linking Storytelling to Your Elevator Pitch

Sometimes—check that, often—you don't have much time to tell your story to busy, short-attention-spanned high school students.

That's where the *elevator pitch* comes into the picture.

If you haven't heard of an elevator pitch before, you can probably surmise what it is from the name. Simply put, it's an opening sales pitch that is succinct enough to give on a trip down the elevator with a client. The effectiveness of an elevator pitch relies on the salesman's ability to encapsulate everything he's trying to sell into a quick, easy-to-follow spiel. At the end of the pitch, ideally the listener should know what the salesman is selling and why he needs to buy it. In other words, during the time it takes him to go down the elevator, he should go from complete stranger to potential customer.

Though the term "elevator pitch" may evoke visions of business suits and briefcases, the ability to give a snappy, polished opening pitch at a moment's notice is a crucial skill in collegiate storytelling circles. Think of the novice screenwriter who is able to corral a top producer for a quick walk down the street or the sports agent who has to espouse the benefits of his free agent client to thirty different teams. If you're in the business of selling your college to high school kids, the first thing you need to be able to do is explain to young *consumers* why they should care about your college and campus. And you have to do this within an extremely short window of opportunity.

> ### Elevator Pitch Defined
>
> The term "elevator pitch" is used a lot in Hollywood—and in business.
>
> Quite simply, an elevator pitch is akin to pitching a two-hour film in a couple of minutes. It must be brief yet far more specific than the sweeping goals of a codified mission statement. "Deliver world-class education" or "value-added studies" isn't sufficient—an elevator pitch needs to say "how" and "why" in a few words to elicit a distinct response.

There are many postsecondary schools in this country that don't have the benefit of a one-word sales pitch like "Harvard" or "Princeton" to keep students lining up outside the gates. For those schools an elevator pitch—just a condensed story—is one of the best ways to get students interested in what they have to offer.

Though theories on elevator pitches abound, most follow a basic structure that strategically unveils the key information you're trying to get across to the client. There are four major points you must address.

- **Who you are** I talked about the *who you are* earlier in this chapter. Do not assume everyone knows who you are. Try to form a quick synopsis of the school using minimal but informative descriptors: "ABC College is a selective liberal arts college of 3,000 passionate students located on a scenic 30-acre campus 10 miles south of Major City."

- **What you do** What makes your college intriguing to the listener? Certainly your school doesn't just teach students; maybe instead it "challenges and inspires students." Whereas other schools offer a list of majors, your college provides "72 diverse and rigorous programs." Get creative, but don't stray off course.

- **What makes you unique** Take *what you do* a step further by specifically stating what makes your school different and thus worth hearing more about. Utilize key statistics and accomplishments to bolster this part of the pitch, but don't go too heavy on numbers or obscure awards. The idea is to categorically distinguish your school in a way that will be understood by the listener. I'll touch on this point more later.

- **What you can do for the listener** This is the crucial sales pitch, the point at which you bring the listener into the big picture you've quickly established.

Visualize Your Story

Should your storytelling have a "look" as well as a compelling message? Certainly.

In fact, design has everything to do with how prospective students and parents receive your message. Never forget the power of visual imagery, especially for a media-saturated generation of high school students. The look and feel of your campaign reveal as much about your stories as the copy. Design in print or on-screen must capture the style of your school, which requires professional photography that works seamlessly as an extension of your brand. As part of the big picture, design works to tell stories that give prospective students a sense of place and of how they might belong there.

Elevator Pitch as Tagline

These days, the most common form of an elevator pitch in academia is via a *tagline*.

Just about every college has a tagline, and taglines are a good way to send an "elevator" message. Each describes, in a sentence or so, the supposed heart and soul of the school in question. But many are not authentic, and some are downright just trying to be cute.

In my research for this book, I ran into a blog post on college branding from a pretty smart guy named Lou Caravella of Vital Communications.

Lou found a website called HigherEdTaglines.com, which claims to index 3,500 taglines for U.S. colleges and universities. Created by Richard Harrison Bailey/The Agency, the site allows schools to update their tagline if it is out-of-date or incorrect.

Here are a few of the taglines analyzed by Lou, along with his often acerbic but accurate comments.

- Miami University, Oxford, OH: *For Love and Honor.* Sounds like a rallying cry from *Braveheart* but definitely purposeful.

- Bowling Green State, OH: *Changing the world by degrees.* A few schools use puns involving "degree" and the less heavy-handed ones seem to work better. South Georgia College, for example, uses *A Degree of Difference.* These two taglines, particularly Bowling Green's, say something meaningful independent of the play on words.

- University of Alaska, Fairbanks: *Latitude with Attitude.* This slogan would be great for a tourist destination in Fairbanks or for Fairbanks itself. Not sure how well it does for a university. The school also uses the slogan "America's Arctic University" and "A 360+ Million-Acre Classroom." They're really running with this tourist angle. An effort for out-of-state applicants?

- Notre Dame: *Nowhere but Notre Dame.* This tagline works insofar as it suggests Notre Dame is like no place else on earth. To students who are apprehensive about attending a school in a rural setting (i.e., in the middle of nowhere) this slogan might be less helpful.

- Montreat College: *Christ-Centered Student-Focused Service-Driven.* Succinct and strong.

- Princeton University: *Princeton in the nation's service and in the service of all nations.* From what I can tell, this is one of the few non-religious schools that emphasize *service* in its tagline, just as Harvard is one of the few secular schools that emphasize *truth* through its motto of, well, *Truth* (Veritas, actually). By mentioning service to all nations, Princeton also reminds us of its global stature.

Lou makes good points here (although I expect the city fathers of South Bend might object to Notre Dame's location as "rural").

The larger point is that school taglines are the closest thing a college actually has to an elevator speech. It's a chance to compress all that is good and compelling about a school in just a few words.

My take? I think we have to ask ourselves what the purpose of the tagline is as part of an overall college branding effort. In most cases, the tagline isn't enough to state the brand premise. Rather, it should be consistent with the school's branding and have some kind of emotional payload. For example, I like Notre Dame's *Nowhere but Notre Dame* tagline, as the undergrad experience there is indeed quite unique. The school builds an unusually strong bond with its students (it always ranks in the top few for alumni loyalty), and this is one way to underscore that in a few words. Princeton's service theme with a global perspective strikes a nice note, even if it may not appeal to all of the avaricious investment banking wannabes who (at least in past years) may have aspired to attend the school.

One also has to ask whether a tagline differentiates the school from other institutions in any significant way. I rather like the approach used by the University of Alaska–Fairbanks in all of their slogans, but I particularly like "A 360+ Million-Acre Classroom." For out-of-state students, this sets the school apart from the competition. It may not appeal to all applicants, but as in any branding effort, segmenting the market is a key part of the process.

Should You Test Your Message?

In a white paper titled "Taglines Are Dead," Ryan Millbern of Richard Harrison Bailey points out that many of the slogans adopted by schools mean nothing:

Education. Excellence. Success. Challenge. Change. Future. Discover. Culture. Character.

Do these taglines tell you anything at all about the school? Millbern dismisses these examples as "lifeless husks that do little more than reflect the pool of generalism in which they float."

I believe college branding is all about differentiation and that a good tagline may turn off as many students as it turns on. That's not a problem if the students (and parents) attracted to the tagline are right for the school. After all, these students are far more likely to apply, be accepted, matriculate, and graduate. Millbern makes a similar point when talking about how *not* to develop a tagline.

> Never test your tagline. Let's face it, your institution isn't—and shouldn't be—for everyone, and if your tagline is coherently communicating the character of your institution, it shouldn't resonate with everyone either. Presenting tagline options to a group of prospective students, parents and

alumni is a great way to turn a quirky, compelling tagline into target practice for amateur critics, or worse yet, an exercise in dilution.

I don't completely agree that never testing your tagline is good advice. I do believe
it's best to test your messages with current customers—those that know you best.
We conduct an exercise with clients in which we ask administrators to name a car,
restaurant or retail establishment that best describes their college. Then we ask current students the same question. You would be astonished by the number of times
they are wildly different.

Even most national consumer brands don't try to appeal to everyone but rather craft
a brand message that is specific enough to resonate with their target segment(s). Just
as a college or university can't be everything to everyone, neither should its tagline.

The Advent of the "Twit Pitch"

How's this for an elevator pitch?

"The University of Massachusetts Boston boasts cutting-edge research faculty with a
teaching soul—and 14,000 students from across the globe."

Notice anything unusual about this attempt to capture the essence of UMass Boston?
It's exactly 140 characters. That's not accidental. It happens to be the maximum allowed by microblogging superforce Twitter.

It was one of several "Twit pitches" submitted by college admissions and marketing professionals in response to an edition of Ray Ulmer's, *The Recruitment Minute*,
about how the elevator pitch is being supplanted in many circles by the lightning fast
Twitter pitch.

Here's another one:

"Vancouver's Langara College is Canada's leader in University Transfer studies and
the pathway to the best universities in the country."

The venerable elevator pitch was supposed to force organizations to strip away all
unnecessary details and get to the essence of who they are in just thirty seconds, approximately the time you might share an elevator ride with your intended audience.
But that's too long for many listeners and readers these days, so marketers are adopting a new shorthand inspired by the wildly popular Twitter site.

The beauty of such an approach, say Twitpitch fans, is that it makes you focus on key
aspects of your institution that define its personality and help differentiate it from
competitors.

And that's a good thing for colleges.

Take a Cue from the Corporate World

The best message about knowing who you are comes from Apple and its CEO, Steve Jobs: Apple really fulfilled its promise via its famous tagline *We are changing computing.*

That says it all, to me. The line compels the listener to absorb the enormity of what Apple is doing: changing an industry that actually changes all the time. Anyone familiar with the Apple brand—whether a fan or not—has to admit that the company has departed from the traditional computer company script, and is clearly delighted about doing so.

But Apple isn't the only good example of a strong message. You can also find some good examples of compelling stories in the corporate world—stories that indicate how the power of performance can set the stage for a compelling and persuasive elevator speech.

Take these two examples.

> In 1987, the warehouse club Costco decided to offer skin-on salmon fillets for $5.99 a pound. The salmon team wasn't satisfied. Next, excess parts were removed from the fillets and the price lowered to $5.29. Then came fully trimmed and skinless fillets at $4.99. In their fourth attempt, buyers started importing salmon in bulk and cut the price to $4.79, and on take five, they improved the cut at no extra charge.
>
> Costco created the Salmon Award to recognize outstanding performances by employees and suppliers. Each award, of course, celebrates a new story and creates new lore.
>
> Another company, Medtronic, started as a hobby and grew into a worldwide designer and manufacturer of medical devices. Every year, the firm throws a party for employees, inviting six patients and their doctors to tell how the company's products helped them.

These stories are inspiring, like that of a Parkinson's patient who reversed ten years of physical deterioration by undergoing an implant for deep brain stimulation. "It was literally a miracle," he told employees.

What makes these stories so powerful? Consider these four takeaways:

- Each story gets to the heart and soul of the company.

- Keep it conversational—strive to use a simple, conversational style. Keep it to one page and always focus on the moral of the story .

- Be specific—here is the "authenticity" theme again. Tell your audience what it is you do best.

- Keep it fresh—be dynamic. As more success stories within your school arise, weave them into the fabric of your elevator pitch.

Translating the Pitch into Your Recruiting Mission

In 2009 on a flight home from San Francisco, where Jeff Kallay was speaking about generations to the Associate Staff of the California Teachers Association, he came across an article that I think stressed the ever-increasing importance of authenticity and why it's so relevant to higher education marketing.

It was in the April 2009 issue of *Fast Company* and titled "25 Ways to Jump-Start the Auto Business." One point (of the twenty-five) was written by contributor Mike Hughes, president and creative director of the Martin Agency.

> "I've gotten at least a half-dozen messages from concerned citizens asking, 'Why don't you guys do for the American car industry what you've done for GEICO and Wal-Mart?'
>
> As powerful as advertising and marketing are, they're not going to save the American car industry. What the industry needs is a vision. The kind Bill Gates had for software, Steve Jobs has for Apple, and, yes, Henry Ford had for automobiles. Don't just give us what you think we want; give us what we should want.
>
> Don't keep telling us your cars are every bit as good now as Toyotas or Hondas. That's probably true today, but you've been trying to sell us that line for far too long. Tell us why we should want your cars. If you can't figure out what makes your product special, then it's probably not special. When you do have something to say, market the hell out of it. Boy, would I love to do that campaign."

Lesson: Your tagline isn't your brand; the experience is the brand. Do you have a special student experience? Tell that story!

The takeaway here? Keep it real! Keep it authentic.

The Leadership Factor

The problem with storytelling, especially as it pertains to elevator pitches, is you don't have a whole lot of time to make your point, so it can be difficult to come across as genuine. It is a sales pitch, after all. Instead of trying to sound authentic, the best tactic is to just be authentic—don't pretend your college is anything other than what it is. Avoid citing statistics or accomplishments that make your school sound like MIT's long-lost cousin; just focus on what your school does best. Your delivery—both in speech and writing—should reflect this sincerity. You're making a sell, but you should sound like you're talking about something that you personally and professionally admire. Convey your passion for your college in your elevator pitch.

The final theme you must keep in mind when making your elevator pitch is leadership and vision. This theme is pivotal to the college admissions process on many levels, of course, but it's a concept that should also play into your sales pitch. Why? Because if you don't have a vision to share with your potential student, why should he care in the end?

Keep in mind that when you're discussing leadership and vision in your elevator pitch, you should mention that the students, faculty, and administration all have a role in it—they're all carrying out your college's vision, whatever that may be. At the same time, you should emphasize that there is a top-down leadership as well that is guiding your college toward all the terrific things it's accomplishing. Students want to be part of something great; they want to know there is meaning and a shared goal at the college they attend. That's the experience economy at work again—the idea that students are looking for something more from college than just a degree or a good time.

In your messaging efforts, try to incorporate the theme of leadership and vision into the wrap-up. Widen the world you've been describing in the previous forty or so seconds; *show how your school is changing lives*. The idea isn't to make it sound like college is going to fix the whole world, but your listener should get the sense that there's been a point to your whole spiel.

Understand that the themes listed above don't necessarily have to be covered in your elevator pitch. In fact, they shouldn't. You don't want to sound to the listener as though you're running through a list of bullet points.

The thing to keep in mind with elevator pitches and associated slogans and online missives is that you always want to be true to your school. Authenticity registers with students and families—we know this now, and it will become more apparent as college applications fall in coming years, as has been predicted. Your elevator pitch—whether you give it on a campus tour, in a chat room, or in a video blog—is your first chance to make your school stand out in a crowded field.

In the next chapter, I'll expand on the concept of sending a positive message by showing how the rest of your college admissions department can create a welcoming, constructive environment for the recruiting process. It will take a top-down examination of the way your college does things.

The Four Keys to a Great Message

With the tenets of a strong—and a weak—tagline in mind, let's close the chapter by using them to construct our own unique messages.

It's my belief that perfecting your college's elevator speech is essentially a four-step process.

- **Know who you are** Colleges who sell their schools on the premise of who they are and who they aren't, and not what they want to be, are the colleges that fare best in their recruiting efforts. The real path to success is to start thinking like a business—that is "you won't get our experience anywhere else."

- **Be able to differentiate yourself** In many pockets of the United States colleges—unfortunately—all look the same. From websites to mailers to campus visits, there is no uniqueness, no differentiation. It's an expensive lesson for colleges to learn—if families can't differentiate, they wind up making enrollment decisions based on price.

- **Be authentic** "Inauthenticity" is a huge problem for colleges—and it's commonplace. By inauthentic, I mean colleges that don't really know who and what they are and instead attempt to display themselves as something or someone else. Colleges need to adopt the successful business model that emphasizes they are doing something better than anyone else.

- **Show great vision and great leadership** You need a leader who has a vision. It's good to have shared governance, and to get options from as many people as possible, but it cannot paralyze the process. Colleges need a leader who can say, "Thanks for the advice but we are going in this direction." The problem? Many college presidents want to create consensus—agreement among faculty, administrators, and staff. Is it more important to retain great faculty or to back the president? Answer: success comes from the top—need support for the college president. A good recruiting program stems from a good vision: knowing what makes your school special and knowing where the college is headed, its roots in history, and where it is now.

In the end, the best messages are the ones that are authentic and that resonate with students and their families.

Chapter 4: The Message

Write an elevator pitch for your institution (that doesn't remind you of another institution).

_____

_____

_____

If your institution were a car, restaurant, or retail establishment, what would it be and why?

_____

_____

_____

Ask a group of current students the same question. Write their answers here.

_____

_____

_____

Is there a perception disconnect? _____

The most authentic thing about a college is the people that go (and work) there and the stories they share. Write one short story about your experience at your institution that you can share with a prospective student and family that helps them make a connection.

_____

_____

_____

5

The Leadership

Managers manage within paradigms. Leaders lead between paradigms.
— Joel Barker, futurist

It's become painfully evident that the lack of decision-making and the culture of collegiality and shared governance have forged an academic recruitment environment that resembles an impenetrable castle, complete with alligator-filled moats and a closed drawbridge.

That's exactly why I want to detail the steps university leaders should take to instill a positive, aggressive student recruiting environment that places a priority on a clear, crisp and compelling leadership strategy—and how to convey that strategy down the line.

The need to do so is critical.

- As I said earlier in the book, there is a perfect storm brewing that threatens to drown many colleges and universities.

- The number of students graduating from high school has begun to decline (particularly in the Northeast).

- The most competitive colleges have gone deeper into their wait list than they have in previous years.

- The financial situation of families and college lenders has created a great unknown: will parents and students be able to afford college?

- The cost of running a college—employee benefits (especially health care), energy, etc.—keeps rising.

- The access to information online about your college that is not the "official line."

- The rise of GenXer parents who are questioning return on investment more than any generation before them.

As a leader at your college, what have you done to prepare for the perfect storm?

If the answer is "not much," you're not alone. My sense is that many colleges are thinking they can simply ride this one out like they have done in the past. But while we have had "storms" (in the early 1980s, for example), we haven't seen this unique combination of factors come together all at once.

So, when you and your colleagues get together to plan next year's enrollment and marketing activities, have you thought about the challenges facing your institution? Are you planning on simply trying to weather the storm or have you thought about tackling it head-on?

These are the questions that collegiate decision-makers should be asking themselves.

Two concepts should be at the forefront of your thinking: authenticity and disruption. Are you being authentic in everything you do or are you sticking with the status quo ("we've always done it this way")? Are you shaking things up, disrupting the marketplace with new and innovative approaches that meet the market's needs or are you maintaining a conservative approach by mimicking what others are doing?

Leaders need to get tougher about the realities facing their campuses and the need to institute the kind of change that makes them more competitive.

That's easier said than done.

Many years ago, Ray Ulmer (TargetX's vice president of communications) and I worked together at a medium-sized northeastern university. One year we added to our marketing strategy the goal of coming up with one, universal logo for the school. What we found was that the university actually had twenty-one different versions of its logo being used, with no "number one" version that the school could rally round.

We explained the problem to the college president and he agreed with us. "We do need just one logo," he said. "But it's more trouble than it's worth." His reasoning? The school had become so decentralized, with various fiefdoms in different departments like athletics, the various schools, and the graduate programs (among others), that it would be a Herculean task to agree on any one logo.

My take was that it was a leadership opportunity missed. I wanted the college president to stand up and be the enforcer. I wanted him to stand up and say, "This is what we are going to look like, and this is the way it's going to be."

You wouldn't expect Henry Ford to go along with twenty-one versions of the fabled Ford Motor Company logo, or Steve Jobs to agree to twenty-one versions of Apple's ubiquitous logo. Why should it be any different in academia? After all, both colleges and companies are in the business of selling their brand, their uniqueness and their authenticity, to customers. How can you do that with twenty-one conflicting visual representations of your messages?

That's where leadership comes into the picture. I understand that campus figures don't like being told what to do and that they don't like to rock the boat.

But to really change the way colleges handle their admissions programs you're going to need leaders who stand up and tell their recruiters, "I'll back you up and put out fires for you."

Leaders are those who make decisive moves even when things look the bleakest and when unpopular stances must be taken.

A Tale of Two Leaders

Sometimes perceptions on leadership can upend conventional wisdom. Ray Blunt, writing on the website GovLeaders.org ("Two Leaders, Two Legacies"), cites the story of "two leaders, an ocean apart, who never met, yet whose lives and purpose paralleled each other's in an amazing way. Both men would gain worldwide fame in their day, though today we hardly know the one while we lionize the other man every year."

He is referring to American icon Thomas Jefferson—father of our Declaration of Independence and our nation's third president—and little-known English abolitionist William Wilberforce.

Both Jefferson and Wilberforce had a great deal in common early in their lives—up to the point in their nascent political careers when they each sponsored unsuccessful legislation to abolish slavery. Their lives then took different paths. Wilberforce, one of Britain's most brilliant politicians of the early nineteenth century, sacrificed his political ambitions to persist in a difficult—and ultimately successful—forty-year struggle to end the slave trade and slavery in England and its colonies. Jefferson went on to the presidency and ended up supporting compromises that extended slavery. Why didn't Jefferson persist in the fight against slavery? Why did Wilberforce?

Texas Changes Its Admissions Culture

Bruce Walker, vice provost and director of admissions at the University of Texas, has spoken loudly and proudly—as well he should—about the university's' *top 10 percent solution*, which was rolled out in 1999. The program guarantees admission to all in-state students (who place in the top 10 percent of their high school class) to any school in the University of Texas system. Calling the program a "grand experiment," Walker says that Texas took a bold step and that the university is a good example of how college leaders can overthrow dead cultures by revamping admissions within the culture of a big university.

His point is a valid one. Walker points out that the *Top 10* program has brought a lot of students into Texas colleges who wouldn't otherwise have had a chance. At a 2009 conference at Wake Forest, Walker issued statistic after statistic that show how well those students have succeeded. "Students in low-performing high schools, if given a chance, can succeed in a major college, even when social structures work against them," he said. But most colleges spend their time and money recruiting students at the top end of the income scale, he said. "What would happen if they spent all that time and money recruiting low-income students?"

The probability of students enrolling in college increases as their family income increases, he noted. "It's easy to recruit those students," he noted. "Down at the bottom, there's very little family social capital, so institutions have to make up for that. It takes more energy and assets to lift the poor to college... You can create an economic engine to change that family's future forever. You begin to deliver social capital to people who never had it before."

That's the type of leadership I'm talking about.

Writes Blunt,

One man eventually fulfilled the early promise and headed his government, while the other remained in the legislature for 40 years, never progressing. Over the course of their lives, both men (to use today's terminology) were respected—even honored—*change* leaders, profoundly altering the course of their countries; yet, both would die with no financial resources. So which would be judged by history as the more successful leader? The one who became President or the one who "languished" in Parliament? This is not a simple question to answer.

For on the other side of the ledger, only one persisted in his commitment to abolish slavery and would live to see its legislated end come peacefully two days before he died. The other, before he died, inexplicably worked to extend slavery, belying his often-voiced principles. Then forty years after his death a terrible civil war was fought to end slavery once and for all, taking the lives of over six hundred thousand men.

Of course, Jefferson and Wilberforce were outstanding leaders in their own right; both took risks, both set high goals (and met them), both had clear and compelling visions of what they wanted achieved, and both held themselves and their followers accountable for changing the political landscape—in historic ways.

Teaching Lessons

What can college leaders learn from Jefferson and Wilberforce? As it turns out, plenty.

Specifically, collegiate leaders can learn from visionaries like Jefferson and Wilberforce how to change "dead cultures."

As we discussed in chapter 2, our *change* chapter, that's not so easy. Let's face it: few industries are as steeped in tradition as higher education. The best schools are also usually the oldest. For instance, venerable institutions like Harvard, Yale, and Princeton are famous as much for their long and storied histories as for their continued roles as higher learning centers. Many more colleges throughout the country also cultivate their own unique customs and ways of doing things. It's part of what makes college special.

It's also a policy mind-set that college leaders should throw out the window.

By "changing cultures" I don't mean to say that Harvard and Yale should stop playing each other in football games each November, or that the Michigan marching band should toss their sheet music for "The Victors." But it's time for college leaders to stop pretending that the old conventions are going to help them survive in a new and challenging economy. As the playing field shifts, schools need to be able to adapt, and they can only do that by overthrowing dead culture.

But you can't change anything without strong leadership. The approaches college leaders use, the assumptions they make, don't fit with reality now, and they certainly won't in the future. The challenges facing higher education in the next few years are not just blips on the radar—they indicate a sea change in the way students and families evaluate colleges.

Once you discard the outdated system, the next step is to put in its place an admissions environment that will not just attract applications but also lead to more enrollments. You will see that it takes leadership at the top and a unity of vision to ensure that a school's marketing message reaches recruits. Many colleges are already enacting these changes and seeing positive results.

Tenets of Leadership on College Campuses

To get to the point where Texas and Spelman (see next page) appear to be, where your school is seeing positive results, college leaders need to focus on four key elements: goal setting, communications, decision-making, and accountability. Let's take a look at all four.

Vision/Goal Setting—Where Are We Going?

The very essence of leadership is [that] you have a vision. It's got to be a vision you articulate clearly and forcefully on every occasion. You can't blow an uncertain trumpet.
— Theodore Hesburgh

Any college president or college admissions officer knows that, although goal setting is critical to achieving critical recruitment objectives, it's no picnic.

The fact is, striving to lead your employees through the ordeal of establishing and then achieving their goals may be difficult—but it can also reap significant rewards for you, your employees, and your organization.

The keys are two fold.

1. Leading (but also empowering) your admissions officers and staffers to effectively establish, set, and subsequently achieve your school's recruitment goals.

2. Figuring out how to use your platform as a campus leader to help admissions employees align their personal goals with your organizational goals.

Here are some guidelines and programs you can use to motivate your admissions staffers and help them meet your critical objectives:

■ **Strategic vision and direction** Collegiate admissions decision-makers need to band together to develop a strategic vision and the direction for the admissions program. Make sure to involve all leaders within the organization to help determine what key goals need to be met for organizational success.

Taking the Lead at Spelman College

Arlene Cash, the vice president for enrollment management at Spelman College, speaking at a college admissions conference at Wake Forest in 2009, related the importance of discovering the hidden treasure in an applicant. She points out that, at Spelman, 25 percent of applicants are considered under a special admission program. But Spelman isn't afraid of changing the game by using a variety of unique methods to get to know an applicant and gather information that will reveal more about the student's potential for success than high school GPA or standardized tests. According to Cash, some of the things a Spelman admissions counselor considers includes: an applicant's excitement about attending Spelman and their commitment to enrolling, matriculating through a program, and graduating.

Cash reports that Spelman applicants accepted through this special admissions process see substantial improvements in their GPA from high school and usually graduate in four years.

- **Empower your admissions staffers** By nature, people don't like being ordered around and told what to do. It's much better to provide the tools, show them the process, and then let them set their own goals. Always remember: ownership = greater commitment.

- **Set annual goals** It's perfectly acceptable to work with your admissions staffers to set goals annually, but make sure to review them with your staff at least once a quarter—or even once a month—to evaluate progress and lend guidance where needed.

- **Keep it real** By all means, have formal guidelines and goal assessment periods. But beyond that, go ahead and informally discuss and review progress toward goal achievement with your employees periodically to ensure progress is being made.

- **Use a ladder approach** Show your admissions staff how to set three to five main annual goals for success as individual employees, then for their department, group, or team, and finally for their overall organization. Ensure that each individual understands this need for alignment between individual, group, and organizational goals.

- **Help your staffers help themselves** Admissions staffers have personal goals, too, and college leaders need to recognize that. To leverage all that ambition, show staffers how to set-project and performance-related goals, but remember to set professional development goals as well.

- **Keep employees in the loop** Here's a way to motivate employees and ensure they're meeting their goals. Have them keep track of their own performance measurements. It will motivate them more to track their own progress and will help keep them from feeling like you are micromanaging them.

- **Be a leader, but be involved** College leaders should show a genuine interest in the progress of their employees. If team members don't believe that you care about their goals, they are not going to be motivated to improve their performance or meet their goals.

- **Setting goals is a balancing act** There needs to be a balance between the needs of the college admissions office and the individual admissions staff. Maintaining that balance while driving your team forward is the key to meeting your recruiting goals—and enlivening stale cultures.

Buy-in—Getting People On Board

A crucial factor in leading your admissions department across the finish line is to master the vital communication skills that make leaders effective.

Leaders who communicate properly and frequently—in good times as well as bad—improve performance, get results, and create a successful enterprise. Leadership consultant John Baldoni offers some helpful thoughts and directives based on the styles of some of the world's most influential leaders, from Winston Churchill to Rudolph Giuliani.

Baldoni's message is crisp and to the point. For collegiate leaders to succeed in communicating their messages to admissions staffers, they need to:

- **develop the leadership message:** determine what you want to say and do

- **deliver the leadership message:** get the message across verbally, mentally, and metaphorically

- **sustain the leadership message:** keep the message alive, fresh, and meaningful

Leaders need to do more than stand up and speak; they need to integrate communications into everything they do, address the immediate concerns and issues, and open the door to future dialogue and discovery.

Here are some other ways to get staffers to "buy-in" to the progressive, positive changes you're implementing with your college recruiting program.

■ **Listen up** Your admissions staff has plenty to say, and it's well worth listening to. When pricking up your ears, make sure to focus on the speaker's message and resist distractions. Keep an open mind to others' ideas. Don't tune out if you disagree. Indicate you understand what the speaker said by reframing key points: "Let me be sure I understand correctly. You're saying…"

■ **Manage conflict** People don't necessarily like change—it threatens fiefdoms and triggers anxiety and insecurity among staffers (and this is perhaps doubly true on college campuses). To reassure your admissions department, make sure to identify and involve major stakeholders. Hold one-on-one or very small group discussions early to vent anger. Make sure that everyone knows in advance why meetings are called. Set ground rules that create an "attack-free," safe haven for dialogue. Use nonjudgmental, non-inflammatory language like "I perceive" or "It seems to me." Reiterate that personal attacks and blame aren't constructive. Identify and reiterate common ground or common goals; focus on areas of agreement. Don't force a resolution; it's Ok to agree to disagree.

■ **Keep your cool** As a leader on campus, you're a role model. As an agent of change, you'll be watched closely. When confronted directly on the necessity of change, or the quality of it, respond mindfully rather than reacting emotionally. This requires self-knowledge and discipline, but it allows for much more effective communication. Get a grip on your hot buttons and identify a "keep calm" strategy for when those buttons get pushed.

■ **Keep people in the loop** Don't make the mistake of neglecting feedback or, worse, manipulating it just to avoid conflict—at the expense of clarity—or confrontation. For instance, instead of saying, "Your attitude is bad" or "That just didn't work," say, "When you miss deadlines, then cross your arms and look away when I talk with you, it gives me the impression you don't care about the quality of your work. Can you help me understand this differently?" Don't forget positive feedback; studies show that a high percentage of employees rarely receive positive feedback from their manager.

■ **Be inclusive** Good leaders are visible, and they make sure their teams are visible. Do this by engaging employees from different areas, and encourage everyone to contribute. Ask employees to send you emails regarding their ideas for doing things more effectively and—very important—respond to all queries. Have a dedicated website or chat room where employees and leaders can exchange concerns and ideas. This will provide the group with different perspectives on the issues discussed and help ensure the top-down/bottom-up information flow.

- **Encourage face time** People like to see the man or woman who's leading the charge, so to speak. That's especially true if staffers don't have frequent contact with you; create opportunities to do so. Sincere face-to-face interaction is key: it gives more weight to telephone, email, or print communications between meetings.

- **Reach out for outside opinions** Studies show that the most successful entrepreneurs and leaders know their limitations and seek outside counsel and resources.

College admissions campaigns can easily be derailed if you can't communicate your team's goals and objectives—you won't get the "buy-in" you need to get everyone moving forward as a unit. Check that by honing your message—and staying on top of it throughout the process.

The Importance of Being Decisive

On college campuses, the decision-making process can often be a paralyzing one. The key to transforming the decision-making process—and progress—is to not view it as a singular event that occurs at only one particular point in time. The opposite is true. Decision-making is actually a process fraught with power plays, politics, personal nuances, and institutional history.

That's the premise of a fascinating article by David A. Garvin and Michael Roberto called "What You Don't Know about Making Decisions" *(Harvard Business Review,* September, 2001).

Garvin and Roberto point out that leaders who recognize the "process versus singularity" theme make far better decisions than those who persevere in the fantasy that decisions are events they alone control.

> That said, some decision-making processes are far more effective than others. Most often, participants use an advocacy process, possibly the least productive way to get things done.

> They view decision-making as a contest, arguing passionately for their preferred solutions, presenting information selectively, withholding relevant conflicting data so they can make a convincing case, and standing firm against opposition. Much more powerful is an inquiry process, in which people consider a variety of options and work together to discover the best solution. Moving from advocacy to inquiry requires careful attention to three critical factors: fostering constructive, rather than personal, conflict; making sure everyone knows that their viewpoints are given serious consideration even if they are not ultimately accepted; and knowing when to bring deliberations to a close.

The authors maintain that decision-making is a "job that lies at the very heart of leadership and one that requires a genius for balance: the ability to embrace the divergence that may characterize early discussions and to forge the unity needed for effective implementation."

Garvin and Roberto provide some useful advice for college leaders who might find themselves at a crossroads in their own decision-making strategies.

- **One decision at a time** The authors say that it's a bad idea to "consolidate" several decisions into one "major" one. Their advice? "Break them apart and isolate them so that the team can address them individually. This will narrow the focus of any objections raised so that the discussion is manageable and can be concluded quickly."

- **Be transparent** Transparency is a term that comes from the political world, meaning to keep things open and visible to everyone. Or, as the authors put it, "Successful organizations put decisions in the sunlight." Decisions made behind closed doors, they say, create an environment of speculation—even suspicion.

- **Give the facts** In a word, knowledge is power. To that end, college leaders need to get ahead of the curve and gather the appropriate facts and disperse them throughout the admissions team. "People need data, whether it's research, budgets, timelines. Provide these tools so they don't have to come back and request [them] later," the authors say.

- **Minimize participants** Do emphasize the sharing of information with those who need it (that's the old "need to know" basis made so popular in the U.S. military and covert espionage sector.) "Ask yourself if a person's objection would stop the project. If so, then don't include them," the authors conclude.

- **Be clear about what "yes" means** This essentially means to be direct. Effective leaders are the ones who can communicate in a crisp, concise, and compelling way when issuing a directive or an opinion. As the authors say, "Don't say 'let me know what you think' when you mean 'do you approve this project?'"

- **Record the decision** Make a record of all of the discussions, meetings, and relevant communications made by the admissions manager and staffers. The authors make the relevant point that there is a "reassurance" factor in play when everything is recorded (i.e., not "hidden") and easily accessible by admissions team members. Having good records also clears up misconceptions among team members. A good intranet site is a highly effective way of storing and sharing college admissions information.

Striving for Accountability—Holding
Admissions Staffers Accountable

I'm a big fan of accountability—I was when I was working in college admissions offices and I am now as the CEO of TargetX.

How can you not be? Think about it. If you take the time to set goals, engage employees, and make big decisions, what a shame it would be if you didn't hold yourself—and your team—accountable for the progress (or lack of it) during your college admissions campaign.

Defining accountability is fairly basic—it's all about everyone on your admissions team taking ownership of (i.e., accepting responsibility for) an initiative and making sure results actually happen.

The burden of creating a landscape for accountability rests on collegiate leaders, including the college president and the college admissions director. It's a tricky scenario, in that it's easy for leaders to remove accountability (usually by not following through on initiatives and not accurately assigning roles and responsibilities). When that happens, it's the admissions director and the college president who wind up *accountable*.

There's also a ripple effect to accountability. If you don't demand it, myriad problems can arise including the following:

- underperformance (usually in the form of missed admissions head count goals or net tuition revenue)

- weak customer service and retention issues

- a drift back to that silo-driven, shared governance–dominated culture where each "fiefdom" operates on its own whims, schedules, and timelines

- lack of professional growth for your admissions team and turnover

- additional anxiety for your admissions managers

How can you nip this situation in the bud and restore order to your newly revitalized recruiting campaign?

Try These Steps

- **Be a role model** Remember that the admissions leaders including the college president and admissions director, are always accountable. Once you're accountable, and everyone knows it, it's much easier to transfer "slices" of this accountability to individuals in the work-group. If accountability is not transferred, then employees will potentially put the manager in jeopardy by not keeping their commitments.

- **Encourage your team to own their success** Make no mistake, team members will operate more efficiently and take firmer control of your program if you strive for accountability. Not only will it encourage a climate of accomplishment, team members can also take pride in owning the success that comes with meeting your admissions goals. Simultaneously, team members may become anxious over the ramifications of not meeting program objectives and subsequently fear that the retribution (real or imagined) will be overly negative. Team leaders may counteract this mind-set by shifting emphasis from overemphasizing mistakes to celebrating achievement. Once team members are free from this anxiety, they can step forward and create better results.

- **Don't over manage accountability** Accountability can only work if the team leader crystallizes what the expected outcomes are, frames the boundaries in which the team will operate, and then enables the employees to take ownership of how they meet project goals. A team leader may take the view that assigning job tasks is enough to create accountability. If the team leader delegates a task and dictates how it must be done, then the accountability remains with the team leader. But if the team leader details the desired outcome and then gives team members the latitude to achieve the outcome using their own talents, the employee can be held accountable for results.

- **Take measure** It almost sounds banal, but keeping score is part and parcel a big part of your accountability campaign. Scorekeeping enables team members to show one another and team leaders whether recruiting goals are being met. The scoreboard must be simple enough and visual enough such that everyone can tell at a glance whether they are meeting or missing those goals. Another key benefit is that scorekeeping also taps into peer pressure. Most people do not want to let others down. Having peers be able to see the performance of others gives each person the motivation to succeed and be part of the team.

Also…

- Be clear about the results—student and faculty satisfaction, elimination of wasted effort, safety, housekeeping, and expense control.

- Ask each employee on your team what he or she can do to help improve and positively impact the results.

■ Avoid diluting the accountability—do not take back ownership of the task when the employee finds it difficult. Let him or her grow through the experience.

■ Track progress and allow the team to take credit for achieving the results.

Identify, correct, and potentially weed out the team members who are not capable or motivated to achieve results.

Let's be realistic. When you emphasize accountability, you're going to face some roadblocks, especially from admissions staffers who aren't accustomed to being held accountable for their performance. But encourage accountability just the same.

Wake Forest Reassesses—and Changes For the Better

In her opening remarks to the Rethinking Admissions Conference at Wake Forest University on April 15, 2009, Provost Jill Tiefenthaler talked about how leaders at her university were able to upend conventional wisdom and change the way it recruited students.

Tiefenthaler told her audience that in 2008, right in the teeth of the "Great Recession," Wake Forest began an internal conversation about how to best craft a class of students who will become the thinkers, scholars, and leaders of tomorrow. The school looked at standardized testing, diversity, creativity, and how to evaluate success in college. It discussed some of the issues it was focusing on at this conference: rising inequalities in access to higher education, whether standardized exams measure the potential to succeed, and questions about how to reach a more heterogeneous group of students.

The college decided to take an approach that reflects not only who it was as a community but also who it wanted to be in the future. So they made personal interviews —on-campus, on Skype, and online—a more significant part of the process. It also requested additional essays and short answers, which offered a more revealing glimpse of candidates.

Says Tiefenthaler,

> We made national news by downplaying the role of standardized testing in the selection process. While 28 percent of colleges do not require the ACT or SAT, we were the first nationally ranked university to make the submission of those scores optional.

It's still early, and we will continue to monitor this closely, but so far we've learned a few lessons from our experience.

We've heard from many high-achieving high school students who say they are drawn philosophically to an institution that assesses merit in a broader sense—one that emphasizes intellectual curiosity, creativity, and diversity of viewpoint.

And we are now attracting students from all backgrounds. In a year where applications declined at many private colleges, applications for our freshman class increased by 16 percent. Applications from students of color increased 46 percent; African American applicants, 70 percent; North Carolina applicants, 52 percent; and applications from international students rose by 36 percent.

Has admissions been more difficult to manage? Definitely. The process has been more labor intensive and has required more discussion and deliberation. But we are energized by the experience. We believe that our personal attention and investment in each applicant will result in a class that enriches and enlivens the Wake Forest community.

This is a good example of how leadership can foster change and garner positive results. It's not easy, but showing the way with new initiatives breeds results, and results breed confidence and, ultimately, even better team-wide performance.

Leadership Is All About Changing Dead Cultures

As you probably know by now, we're a bit *edgy* at TargetX—always looking ahead, anticipating the trends, embracing change, and pushing our clients forward. A few years ago we embraced a mantra at TargetX—*overthrowing dead culture*. We have it above our conference room door and even written (in Latin) on the back of black long-sleeve T-shirts you may have received at NACAC or a TargetX event. This phrase isn't something we created—it's a bit of folklore from the humble beginnings of Apple Computer in the 1970s.

As the story goes, and is played out in the made-for-television movie *Pirates of Silicon Valley* staring Noah Wyle as Steve Jobs and Anthony Michael Hall as Bill Gates, Steve Jobs is approached by Mike Markula from Intel. Mike wants to invest in a small computer company. Steve corrects him that they are not a computer company—they are *overthrowing dead culture*. At that time IBM was the "dead culture" Apple was attempting to overthrow.

Which is exactly what happened. Today, Apple's market cap is almost double that of IBM.

Steve Jobs was a leader and he proved it by taking the reins, setting a goal, communicating that goal to his company, and making the decisions necessary to make it happen.

That's what leaders do, and it's what you have to do to overthrow your own college's *dead* culture.

Chapter 5: The Leadership

What are your five professional priorities for this year?

1. _____

_____

2. _____

_____

3. _____

_____

4. _____

_____

5. _____

Is your team aware of these priorities? ❑ Yes ❑ No

Are their priorities aligned with your priorities? ❑ Yes ❑ No

What percent of your time do you spend on a regular basis:

_____ percent at your desk

_____ percent in meetings

_____ percent with your team

_____ percent with your customers

How many different logos is your institution currently using? _____

6

The Team

Never doubt that a small group of thoughtful committed citizens can change the world. Indeed it is the only thing that ever has.
—Margaret Mead

In college admissions, as in any organizational endeavor, identifying your mission is only half the battle.

The other is to create a plan and build a team that will drive you to the finish line.

That's not always easily done. Colleges, by their very DNA, aren't necessarily hotbeds of teamwork and collaboration.

Ask any college administrator how closely he or she works with other university departments and, chances are, you'll get a shrug and some vague answer amounting to "we're doing what we can." Now more than ever, recruiting future students requires taking an "it takes a campus to recruit a student" mentality.

The pervasiveness of the "silo" approach on many college campuses can undermine the potential for collaboration among key departments. According to Evan Rosen, author of *The Culture of Collaboration* and executive director of the Culture of Collaboration Institute, the term "silo" is a metaphor "suggesting a similarity between grain silos that segregate one type of grain from another and the segregated parts of an organization."

Rosen believes that organizations that encounter the silo syndrome suffer the same fate: on a daily basis, each department or function interacts primarily within that "silo" rather than with other groups across the organization. "Marketing may develop its own culture and have difficulty interacting with other functions such as sales or engineering. This manifestation of silo syndrome breeds insular thinking, redundancy, and suboptimal decision-making," he adds.

He issues a warning to colleges and universities that look the other way when their college admissions officers don't collaborate with other departments. "Unless the vendor is the only game in town, the customer may look elsewhere," he offers.

But there are exceptions—and those exceptions are usually schools that plan ahead and merge their goals and guiding philosophies within their teambuilding frameworks.

Take the Ralph C. Wilson, Jr. School of Education at St. John Fisher College. The Rochester, New York, liberal arts school has built a solid reputation around the conceptual framework of social justice. It graduates educators with a unique sense of right and wrong who go on to make a huge difference as teachers in their communities.

The Jesuit school actually has something you don't see every day: a "mission statement" outlining how the school's various departments should work together for the common good.

St. John Fisher College: Teamwork Statement

"Long term success in a work environment can often be predicted based on the level of trust, respect, honesty, humor, integrity, hard work, communication and shared responsibility that is exhibited by its people."

To this end, the faculty and staff in the School of Education have endorsed the following statements to promote teamwork and positive working relationships and to sustain a culture of collegiality:

Behavior

- Listen to and respect each other by recognizing each person's right to disagree and be heard.

- Be loyal to each other and take collective responsibility for our decisions.

- Be open and honest while demonstrating flexibility and sensitivity.

- Honor and support each other's roles, requests, contributions, and needs.

- Stretch our limits while being mindful of our limitations.

- Recognize and celebrate individual and collective successes.

- Accept constructive criticism, suggestions, or inquiries about our work.

- Provide help to each other while being sensitive to individual needs.

- Use data, research, and discussions to inform our decisions.

- Use humor to help keep things in the proper perspective.

Communication

- Share information with each other regularly on actions and the resolution of issues, and follow up with each other accordingly.

- Maintain confidentiality and avoid "leaking" sensitive information with others outside the team.

- Promote and model appropriate use of workplace technology to support frequent and ongoing communication.

Meeting Protocols

- Limit during-meeting cell phone interruptions to "emergency" calls.

- Do not interrupt each other or have "side conversations" while others have the floor.

- Be on time, and start and end meetings on time and stick to the agenda.

My take? A school that values social justice and increased awareness of the power of working together to build better communities knows the value of teamwork—and lives it every day.

In doing so, St. John Fisher vastly increases its chances of avoiding the fate Rosen describes.

With St. John Fisher's blueprint on team play, I bet that college students won't be as likely to "look elsewhere" after they visit the campus.

I think that having a teamwork message officially spelled out—right there on the college president's letterhead and with the school's logo attached—is a powerful motivator, especially for the college admissions office. In my experience, college admissions departments don't always work in harmony with other departments (particularly marketing).

I understand the point that admissions directors and marketing directors make:

- The admissions director: "Hey, we're the gatekeepers and the tip of the spearhead for our schools. It's our job to recruit the right students and fill those classrooms. Money is the lubricant that makes any college run from a productivity point of view, and we're the ones who bring it in. So don't get in our way—we know what we're doing."

- The marketing director: "Hold the phone. The marketing department builds the brand that, over the long haul, brings in the students year after year. Without us, the admissions team would have nothing to sell."

Unfortunately, college admissions and marketing departments that work seamlessly together are a rare occurrence. Our team at TargetX has visited way too many college admissions departments and held meetings where there was nobody from marketing in attendance. When we do talk to marketing people they tell us that they don't trust the admission's department to get the right message out to prospective students and their families. But when we talk to the admissions staff they act very much like a corporate sales unit, telling us that it is admissions who really tap into what students really want.

Consequently, turf battles over things like social messaging campaigns or uniform logo designs crop up all the time between the two departments.

At the Rochester Institute of Technology (RIT), the New York–based school brought together marketing, admissions, and a host of other key university departments to recraft its brand as a high-quality, career-focused technological school. But the key ingredient in the image-rebuilding campaign was that marketing and admissions worked together. In a white paper produced by the Council for Advancement and Support of Education (CASE) titled "Communications Is from Mars, Admissions Is from Venus," senior vice president of enrollment management at RIT Jim Miller said, "If marketing and admissions are too far apart, the university can't realize its full potential. It won't leverage what it has as quickly or as well."

Identifying three key tenets that I've talked about all along in this book—leadership, structure, and talent—the RIT rebranding campaign honed in one simple message that every department adopted and pushed out to the public: that RIT was a destination point for talented, technology-savvy high school students both here in the United States and abroad.

"All communication starting from the same premise is good," added Miller. "It helps the university focus and prioritize to be consistent with its strategic plan." The RIT rebranding campaign, launched in 1984, has since led to a significant uptick in quality students from around the world.

What the various departments at RIT learned (especially in the marketing and admissions departments) is that united behind one goal, and with good leadership and communication, teambuilding is light-years better than the old "silo" approach.

And that's a win-win for everybody.

Doing Good by Doing Well—As a Team

Tennessee-based South College has a unique way of instilling teamwork in its admissions department.

The school sent its admissions department out into the field—literally—to help Habitat for Humanity's Urban Garden (HUG) Foundation create a local community garden called Beardsley Farms.

The farm produces fresh vegetables, fruit and flowers for citizens in and around Mechanicsville, Tennessee. Much of the produce goes to poor families and food pantries in the community.

How did the South College admissions team help out? Steven A. South, president of the college, spells it out for us:

"There is no better way to promote departmental teambuilding than by working together on a project that brings you back to something as basic as growing food," South explained. "Our team pulled weeds, pushed wheelbarrows, built compost bins, planted plants, and earned praises from the HUG staff for making a difference."

South singled out Anna Rosetti, who was among the group of more than a dozen South College team members who cleared brush and laid out a fresh, new patch of fertile land for the farm to grow more produce. "They spent a long morning clearing that plot of land. In spite of being extremely sore the next day, Anna said it was great to work together on a project outside the office. They learned a lot about gardening and discovered a different side of one another. Anna also mentioned how rewarding it was to give back to the community."

Taking your team outside the office is a good example of how college admissions teams can learn to work more closely together—in the case of South College, very much altruistically so.

One Plan, Many Hands Working Together

As St. John Fisher and RIT already know, the secret to success is teamwork.

The colleges understand that communicating openly and frequently with employees is critical for success. Most college admissions understand that everything "matters." In fact, most college admissions' internal communication plan revolves around this concept: everything that every employee does, every experience on campus or regarding the campus, speaks volumes to its customers about "who we are."

Therefore, again and again we see college admissions officers try to communicate to everyone at the university that each employee is part of something greater. The way that someone in financial aid answers the phone, for example, is indicative of the quality of the college community. The way a groundskeeper cares for the century-old live oaks on a campus or the way a custodian maintains a historic building reflects the care schools take and the pride they have in their institutions. Everyone plays a critical role in advancing the university's strategic priorities.

In that regard, colleges have more in common with traditional businesses—a lot more in common—than they might think.

That's true in myriad ways, from sales and marketing to customer service, and it's especially true concerning the key theme in this chapter: teamwork.

There's no getting around it: you won't get anywhere in college admissions unless you have key university departments working in sync with one mission, one plan, and a unified sense that we're all in this together.

From our experience at TargetX working with many schools nationwide, however, success stories are an exception rather than the rule.

In fact, one thing that stops colleges from reaching their college admissions goals is the embedded, anti-business culture that permeates university campuses. John Lombardi, president of the University of Massachusetts at Amherst, got it right when he said that "universities for the most part do not have management; they have governance." To Lombardi, that means "the political process that balances the various competing interests of an institution through a complicated and lengthy process."

His point is a good one—that governance of the shared variety is indeed an impediment to action because it has the tendency to replace progress with process, which often means that action will be endlessly deferred. Lombardi concludes, "To improve, the university must have management. It must have direction. The institution must consult ... must listen, and it must respond to ... advice from its many constituencies, but it must nonetheless act, and often it must act without complete consensus."

That's the premise of teamwork, whether it's at a manufacturing plant or at an Ivy League college admissions office. But at a manufacturing plant, the end game is not to define the goal but to meet it, whereas colleges are forever mired down in defining the job and establishing processes and pecking orders. In doing so, the job at hand might ultimately not get done.

Stanley Fish, writing for *Change* magazine ("Shared Governance: Democracy Is Not an Educational Idea"), points out that the difference between management and shared governance is that management is, by and large, aware of its instrumental status—it does not define the job but helps get it done. Fish's message is worth listening to for any collegiate leader looking to build an effective admissions team—and avoid being thwarted by hierarchical politics.

There is still another way in which academic life differs from the life of business. In the business world, those at the top of the organizational hierarchy are regarded (not only by themselves but by others lower on the food chain) as the key players and the ones best positioned and equipped to make the important decisions.

In the academic world, by contrast, subtle power plays and territorial, turf skirmishes may work their way into the process, especially between faculty and college admissions and marketing departments. Each department needs each other, but each department is wary of each other.

The organizational chart of a university may suggest that authority rests with the administrators, who, as the management class, set the standards to which faculty, the labor class, must conform. But faculty do not think of themselves as labor (hence the resistance to unionization) but are convinced—a conviction that seems to be issued to them along with the Ph.D.—that authority really rests with them and that the hierarchy announced in the organizational chart is a fiction they are in no way obliged to respect.

I once explained this to someone, who then asked, "Well, if they think that, why don't they assume the positions in the hierarchy themselves?" The answer is that they believe that such grubbing after administrative power is beneath them.

Fish is on to something. There's a strong connection, just like links in a steel chain, between changing cultures in college admissions and changing the way admissions efforts are constructed.

From my experience, one of the most compelling reasons why college admissions programs don't reach their goals and don't connect with students and families is teamwork—or more specifically, the lack of it.

Of course, academia doesn't have a monopoly on teambuilding challenges. Any industry—in fact, just about any endeavor—relies on a group of qualified individuals who communicate well, build consensus, and support each other in meeting team goals.

That's the way it should be. Because in teambuilding, everyone has a distinct and important role—and that's something that colleges and universities don't always understand.

Consider this story. A sea captain and his chief engineer got into an argument about which one was more important to the ship. Finally they decided to swap jobs for a day.

The chief went up to the bridge and the captain went down to the engine room. After a few hours, the captain suddenly appeared on deck, covered with oil and soot.

"Chief!" he yelled, wildly waving a monkey wrench. "You'll have to come down here! I can't make her go!"

"Of course not!" said the chief. "We're aground."

A lot of college admissions programs are aground, too—but this is a ship, in total, that can be righted and can sail again.

Putting Paralysis in its Place

As a marketing executive, I know the power of teamwork. As a collegiate marketing executive, I know how easy it is for academically themed teams to get bogged down in paralysis, as members talk plenty and decide nothing.

That's where the college president must step in. An effective leader needs to set deadlines and make the team live up to those deadlines.

Don't get me wrong. Informed discussion and consensus are key goals of any college team. But sooner or later, you're going to have to make a tough call.

Knowledge + Communications = Good Teamwork

It's no secret that one of the most important things collegiate leaders can do to get that process started is to build a great admissions team.

It's no mystery why. Working as a team in the college recruiting market is just as important as it is for a manufacturing team at Ford or the iPhone team at Apple.

Left alone, especially in the silo culture that can permeate academia, the impossible remains impossible.

But when admissions staffers work as a team, the impossible becomes entirely possible.

That's why, in academic admissions, the difference between successful programs and failed ones is the relative strength and capabilities of the college recruiting team. By "teamwork," I don't mean focusing only on how to find the best people but also on establishing a program that gets the most out of each team member's capabilities.

After all, there's a lot on the line for colleges, especially in a recruiting environment where competition is fierce and success is measured in the color of the ink that makes up your bottom line. Couple that with the economic environment where information is as much a commodity as widgets or washing machines.

In my two-plus decades in the college admissions game, I've come to believe that the number one service that colleges can provide for students and families (and each other) is good, solid, useful information. Study after study bears this out. Students and families want—make that crave—information on admissions, financial aid, curriculum, athletics, and other issues that will impact their decision about what college to attend.

Providing information makes a big difference for colleges and universities. Colleges that fail to provide key information are the colleges that miss recruitment opportunities (and worse, miss retention goals for existing students).

Ultimately, that failure comes down to a failure of teamwork.

Let me elaborate. Besides the "shared governance" syndrome that I mentioned above, there is no shortage of reasons why colleges are limited in their ability to successfully get the right information to prospective candidates. For starters:

- Information resides primarily in the heads of specialized administrative staff, so the ability to answer questions is constrained by the availability of those specialists.

- Information is dispersed across multiple independent offices, forcing students to look in several places before finding someone or something that can answer their questions.

- Administrative offices typically handle communications on an ad hoc basis, so there is little consistency or synergy between the answers students are given on the phone, via email, or on the web.

■ Budgets for phone support, email management, and web content development are limited, undermining communications capabilities across all channels.

Teamwork Tips Bearing Down at Baylor University

At TargetX, when we advise admissions departments, we often stress the importance of the three T's—talent, training, and tools—when embracing change in recruiting students today. But there is actually a fourth T, teamwork, without which the other three qualities are unlikely to gain any real traction.

A prime example of exceptional teamwork is Baylor University, in Waco, Texas. The school is a destination point for high school students all over the world and has about 14,000 students enrolled each year.

Baylor is very good at getting the types of kids the school wants—bright, creative thinkers who will likely move on to become socially minded engineers, doctors who run their own practice, or entrepreneurs ready to start a business of their own someday. (For inspiration, an entrepreneurially minded student only has to look across town at the corporate headquarters of Dr. Pepper, which was founded in Waco.)

To find such students, Baylor's admissions department pays special attention to the management needs of the staff to create a high-performance, innovative team. They have discovered that with Millennials, the best model is a cohort management system allowing them to work in dedicated teams to relate to and recruit the ideal Baylor student.

"Teamwork is one of the most important elements in the recruitment process," notes Jessica King Gereghty, director of admissions counseling and recruitment at Baylor. "The first thing we look for in an interview is the candidate's ability to work in a large team. When we interview a person and they start to talk about being a strong leader, we ask clarifying questions to further explore if this candidate can be an employee who is part of a team and who wants to be part of something bigger than themselves."

Actually, that's not as difficult as it might sound. "We have been hiring lots of Millennials in our admissions department, and they do want to be part of a team," adds Jennifer Carron, assistant vice president of admissions services at the school. "We've found that Millennials naturally gravitate toward teams-based professional development and management. It's an inherent part of their culture."

Baylor breaks down its counseling and recruitment team into cohorts according to their level of experience: first-year, second-year, and veteran admissions counselors. Several years ago, a new group of counselors began a tradition in the office of selecting a cohort team name. Here's a look at the current team names: The newest arrivals to the admissions team (first-year's team) are still debating a group identity, but one we keep hearing in the halls is the Arctic Puffins. The second-year staffers are all on a team called the Feisty Squirrels; and the more experienced third-year counselors are known as the Wild Boars.

"Millennials grew up on teams in middle school and in high school so they're used to what we do," says Gereghty. "Altogether we have about twenty-five staffers in our counseling and recruitment team and individual, weekly appointments for each member for a team this size is not a fruitful use of time. But by breaking down the department into groups, we can meet with them more often to discuss goals, evaluate progress, and make changes if we have to."

Gereghty points to "tent week," which comes at about the same time as spring break every year. It's typically the most heavily trafficked time of the year in terms of high school kids visiting the campus. Consequently, it's all hands on deck for the admissions department, and their team concept really pays off all week.

"We set up a big tent right at the front entrance to the campus," she adds. "Last year, the Boars planned the whole campaign from start to finish. They made sure the entire operation had the tools we needed to help our visitors get the most from their experience on campus—everything from setting up outdoor offices to food permits and approval from the local fire department. They worked together as a team and got the job done."

The tent theme has been a big success for Baylor, but Gereghty notes, it's the team concept that keeps the engine running. "It's definitely made a difference," she says. "We usually have two to three times more visitors than normal, but the Boars made it seem like things were running smoothly. We take deposits right in the tent and have seen improvement in our numbers—we'll have a record enrollment this year. Plus, with a team focus on customer service and creativity, our visitors are sure to have an exciting on-campus experience they won't quickly forget."

No doubt, Baylor has found a winning format in their admissions department built around the concept of teamwork. "Working together as a team helps our staff of young professionals know they are progressing together toward a goal, and they know that college admissions could be a great career for them," Gereghty says. "But what really counts is that they see themselves moving forward as a team. That's what we're looking for."

Choosing Good Team Members

What makes a good collegiate admissions team member?

Choosing the right admissions team member is a tough but necessary chore. The qualifications have changed, having moved from a traditional, administrative role to a more sales and marketing-driven role, with a healthy dash of social networking skills tossed into the mix.

Team members also have to deal with budget shortfalls, a rise in first-generation students, and increased demands by students and families for vigorous and compelling academic programs. You'll want team members who can hit the ground running and make an immediate impact. They should all have a keen competitive edge, be able to act proactively and independently, offer robust communication skills, possess personal experience with the financial aid process, and have absolutely no tolerance for the shared governance culture of ambiguity and indecision.

Let's have a look at some of these crucial qualities.

Independence College team members are able to execute tasks on their own, provided they are given the correct data and tasks to execute. When reviewing team member qualifications, look for examples of workplace independence on résumés and in interviews. For example, anyone who has ever traveled overseas or started a business can likely be counted on in unsupervised projects.

Make no mistake, even members of workplace teams sometimes operate in isolation. You want people who excel in doing so.

Good communicators Obviously, a good collegiate admissions officer must be able to talk, influence, and persuade. But it's not all about talking one-on-one with students and parents. A high premium should be placed on writing skills, social networking skills, and email and phone correspondence. Ask candidates to provide samples of written correspondence. Check their handshake for firmness. Strive to find good listeners and those who make good eye contact—it only takes a moment for a prospect to make a decision about whether to attend your school.

Savvy at finance With college funding down, finding team members with an affinity for financial aid and who know the ropes on getting students help with college aid is paramount. Look for creative types who have had experience in securing their own funding as a college student. Communicators with a solid financial background are at the top of the list of good candidates for college admissions team members.

The patience of a saint No doubt about it, the university recruiting admissions process is confusing and complex, and dealing with high school juniors and seniors presents its own challenges. Good college admissions team members must stay positive and be able to sympathize with students and families. They must also show tolerance for all types of questions and be sensitive to changes in plans, indecision, and last-minute deviations.

Building Team-Focused "Knowledge Bases"

Corporations understand the need to extend the knowledge base from the inside out—spreading information through the organization and customizing that knowledge for optimum impact within key groups and teams within that organization.

But colleges are different from corporations in some ways. Specifically, they need to get the right information through the right channels to the right audience—the prospective students and families I keep talking about.

It's all about transferring knowledge to customers—when they want it and how they want it. That's the meat-and-potatoes message from a white paper called "Winning Service Strategies for Colleges and Universities" by customer service specialist Right-Now Technologies.

The white paper asks us to consider the corporate customer service center and how it differs from the way colleges reach out to "customers."

Unlike corporate contact centers—which use large numbers of first-tier service/support generalists—colleges and universities generally rely on subject-matter specialists to answer questions. These administrative employees have accumulated a wealth of knowledge over the years about programs, policies, and processes. That makes them great resources for students and parents with questions. However, this approach also means that valuable knowledge remains "locked in the heads" of these key specialists. A school's ability to answer questions is therefore largely constrained by their personal availability.

Colleges and universities also typically interact with their constituencies in a more fragmented way than do corporations. For example, the paper says that a student has to decide whether to call financial aid, the registrar, the bursar's office, the athletic department, or admissions to get information. Even at schools that have implemented some sort of information clearinghouse, these separate departments still maintain a good deal of independence in terms of how they manage and deliver. This can be problematic for students and parents, who may not know exactly which department to talk to and end up contacting several departments to ask multiple unrelated questions.

As the paper practically insists, colleges have that age-old problem associated with hierarchical, silo-based organizations: one hand doesn't know what the other hand is doing.

Corporate contact centers usually have highly structured processes for answering questions, sharing knowledge, and escalating queries. Because of the structure and culture of most educational institutions, such formalized processes usually don't exist.

One department may try to handle every phone call that comes in. Another may ask callers to email their questions so they can be handled later.

Universities can't afford to hire legions of call center operators or the telecom infrastructure those operators need to do their jobs. They can't spend a lot of money on fancy websites or on content development for those sites. They don't have budgets for scaling up their email management capacity.

These resource limitations make it difficult for them to deliver the kind of responsive, high-quality customer service that students need and expect. Despite these apparent hurdles, colleges and universities need to find a way to deliver better service. No one wants to lose a potentially great student because a parent couldn't get a question about financial aid answered. And no one wants to lose an existing student because of a course registration or housing snafu.

The good news—and there is good news here—is that some colleges are beginning to change their silo-based models and are learning to share information among dedicated admissions teams that, when banded together, can create information-driven capabilities that get the right information to the right prospect at the right time, thus significantly enhancing the chances of signing that prospect up on the bottom line.

Teamwork and Knowledge Flow at the University of Oklahoma

Like RIT and South College, some colleges get the message about teamwork. The University of Oklahoma has done so by creating information delivery programs that depend on the distinct talents of team members to communicate quickly and accurately with prospects.

Sharing critical information, managed by dedicated teams, is at the heart of the University of Oklahoma's successful Financial Aid Services program.

If there's one set of departments that must work more closely together today it is admissions and financial aid. They need to be a seamless set in the eyes of the prospective family.

The Financial Aid Services is a busy place. The university estimates it can get up to one thousand calls and thousands more in emails over the period of one month. In 2002, the department had only seven employees, tasked with the burden of answering calls that required answers from myriad departments. To streamline the program, the university created an online knowledge center and retrained the staff to come up with twenty-five common questions that students and families were asking—and then to set about reaching out across the campus to answer those questions.

Within weeks the program was up and running, and the team had developed a script with answers to the twenty-five questions—all answers culled from the appropriate departments and offices. Customer satisfaction levels rose, and the financial services team decided to build on the program's success by expanding, within one year of the program's rollout, the knowledge base to 250 questions, thus ensuring even greater customer satisfaction among students and families.

The program's impact also had a positive effect on department staffers. With their phone and email workloads reduced by hundreds a day, office staff now give clients the full attention they deserve. They've also been freed to attend to the quality control measures necessary to ensure financial aid flows to students in a timely manner. In fact, during periods of peak activity, the department's director estimates the system has allowed over 140 person-hours a week to be redirected from answering routine questions to fulfilling critical administrative responsibilities.

How to Set the Stage for Success

Of course, establishing teambuilding campaigns for colleges is a unique proposition, significantly different than for, say, companies in the technology, manufacturing, or auto industry. While these industries build products—good products—colleges and universities have a different aim: to build young adults and send them off confidently into the working world as future leaders and managers.

In reality, teambuilding in colleges resembles the teambuilding strategies in the U.S. military. Think about it. Both colleges and the military focus on young adults. They both instruct; they both open new horizons; they both build character, confidence, and leadership skills.

To actually achieve those goals, both colleges and the armed forces have to build the kinds of teams that can connect with their young charges. Colleges, like the military, need instructors, motivators, psychologists, marketers, sales experts, organizers, and yes, leaders—and that's just on the admissions team.

Even more so, effective teambuilding can change the "dead culture" that so permeates the annals of academia simply by turning departments that were historically operating independently of each other into seamless, cohesive units—all operating in lockstep with one another.

Forming College Admissions Teams

How do we define "team"? Its origins come from our agrarian ancestors, who literally strapped teams of oxen together to streamline the process of transporting heavy loads.

The Power of Mistakes

I've learned that mistakes can often be as good a teacher as success. —Jack Welch

You have to embrace mistakes. People who have the power to make mistakes are those who create great things.

In more contemporary terms, a team is a group of people striving for a common goal, for example, finding a cure for a disease, winning the World Series, or, in our case, reaching out and attracting the students that are a good fit for a university. On teams, individuals contribute to the collective good—think of a pride of lions that work together to bring down a water buffalo or a swarm of bees collecting nectar for the hive. Even in the animal world, teambuilding—make that especially in the animal world—teambuilding is a matter of life and death. It's not so in the college admissions world, although in my experience it sure can feel like it, especially today.

Undertaking Teambuilding

Building the perfect college admissions team is similar to what African lions experience in the open savannah: an ongoing process, fraught with risks and dangers, that ultimately helps a group of individuals evolve into a cohesive unit.

The building blocks to teambuilding involve a step-by-step approach that sets goals and expectations and establishes ground rules for reaching those objectives. Here's a list of steps you can take to establish such practices for admissions teams at your college.

Explain the plan You need to lay out your plan, clearly, concisely, and compellingly, of what you expect in terms of team performance and expectations. Ask yourself these questions: Do team members understand why the team was created? Is your college admissions team supported with key resources like staffing, technology infrastructure, time, and money? Is the work of the team a top-of-the-line priority? To launch a successful college admissions teambuilding program, you'll need to answer these questions—then explain the answers to your staff.

The big picture Do all admissions team members know what's at stake? Do they understand how the strategy of using teams will help your school meet and surpass its admissions goals? Does your team understand where its work fits in the total context of the college's goals, principles, vision, and values? If you can't sell the big picture, then you likely won't be able to sell your admissions team.

All-for-one, one-for-all Do team members actually want to participate on a team? The modern university culture isn't exactly rife with examples of seamless organizational success stories. In my research for this book, finding case studies and success stories about collegiate admissions teambuilding was generally a fruitless chore. Colleges tend to prefer a silo approach to departmental structure where fiefdoms are fiercely protected and other departments tend to be regarded with suspicion and distrust. That "nobody tells me what to do" mind-set is pure poison to effective team collaboration practices. To generate a more palatable environment for a team culture, strive to ensure that team members feel that the team's mission is a vital one. Make sure that team members are committed to accomplishing the team mission and meeting your college admissions programs' expected outcomes. If your team members perceive their service as valuable to the organization and to their own careers, they'll climb aboard that much faster.

Define the team you want to build Teambuilding requires good, strong leadership—right from the top. Don't do this via teambuilding "workshops" or retreats. Most participants don't get anything out of such ventures. Better to define the team you want to build through your vision of what you want your team to be. Focus on goals and objectives and how you want your team to get there.

Professionalism Does the team feel that it has the appropriate people participating? (As an example, in a college admissions process improvement, is each step of the process represented on the team?) Does the team feel that its members have the knowledge, skill, and capability to address the issues for which the team was formed? If not, does the team have access to the help it needs? Does the team feel it has the resources, strategies, and support needed to accomplish its mission?

Holding people accountable

You can't hold committees or task forces accountable. You can only hold individuals responsible.

Individual responsibilities Has the team taken its assigned area of responsibility and designed its own mission, vision, and strategies to accomplish all goals? Has the team defined and communicated its goals; its anticipated outcomes and contributions; its timelines; and how it will measure both the outcomes of its work and the process the team followed to accomplish their task? Does the leadership team or other coordinating group support what the team has designed?

Provide the tools for the job Yes, college budgets are tight, particularly at smaller public colleges. But you should make every effort to squeeze some money out of the budget for technology tools like cell phones, laptops, Internet access while on the road, and CRM software, all of which help team members stay in touch and do a better job of servicing students and families. The shortest distance between two points is

> ## Power Up!
>
> Information is power. Empower your team with financial information in particular.

a straight line, and these days, that line is defined by technology tools.

Empowerment Does your team feel free to take the steps necessary to accomplish its goals? At the same time, do team members clearly understand their boundaries? How far may members go in pursuit of solutions? Are limitations (i.e., monetary and time resources) defined at the beginning of the project before the team experiences barriers? Is the team's reporting relationship and accountability understood by all members of the organization? Has the organization defined the team's authority? To make recommendations? To implement its plan? Is there a defined review process so both the team and the organization are consistently aligned in direction and purpose? Do team members hold each other accountable for project timelines, commitments, and results? Does the organization have a plan to increase opportunities for self-management among organization members?

Communication Are team members clear about the priority of their tasks? Is there an established method for the teams to give feedback and receive honest performance feedback? Does the organization provide important business information regularly? Do the teams understand the complete context for their existence? Do team members communicate clearly and honestly with each other? Do team members bring diverse opinions to the table? Are necessary conflicts raised and addressed?

Creative innovation Are the college and its leaders really interested in change? Do they value creative thinking, unique solutions, and new ideas? Do they reward people who take reasonable risks to make improvements? Or do they reward the people who fit in and maintain the status quo? Do they provide the training, education, access to books and films, and field trips necessary to stimulate new thinking?

Consequences Do team members feel responsible and accountable for team achievements? Are rewards and recognition supplied when admissions teams are successful? Is reasonable risk respected and encouraged in the organization? Do team members fear reprisal? Do team members spend their time finger-pointing rather than resolving problems? Is the organization designing reward systems that recognize both team and individual performance? Is the organization planning to share gains and increased profitability with team and individual contributors? Can contributors see their impact on increased organization success?

Coordination Are teams coordinated by a central leadership team that assists the groups to obtain what they need for success? Have priorities and resource allocation been planned across departments? Do teams understand the concept of the internal customer—the next process, anyone to whom they provide a product or a service?

Are cross-functional and multidepartment teams common and working together effectively? Is the organization developing a customer-focused, process-focused orientation and moving away from traditional departmental thinking?

Cultural change Does the college recognize that the team-based, collaborative, empowering, enabling organizational culture of the future is different than the traditional, hierarchical organization it may currently be? Is the college planning to change (or in the process of changing) how it rewards, recognizes, appraises, hires, develops, plans with, motivates, and manages the people it employs? Does the college plan to use failures for learning and support reasonable risk? Does the college recognize that the more it can change its climate to support teams, the more it will receive in payback from the work of the teams?

Tenets of Successful Teambuilding

By and large, your teams are most effective when:

- a diverse group of employees "buys in" to your team concept—and is eager to participate

- employees are limited to one committee at a time (one employee spread out on multiple teams is a blueprint for confusion—and failure)

- your academic team meets regularly—at least once per week

- specific quantitative goals are set—for example, five hundred new students admitted who fit well within your college culture

- team members are kept in the loop (provide minutes or notes from meetings as well as online forums dedicated to your admissions team)

- your teams self-perpetuate by constantly adding new employees

Happier Admissions Staffers

Sharing the load via workplace teams is not only better for reaching out to students and families, it makes college admissions employees happier, too.

By emphasizing teambuilding, with an equal emphasis on work-life balance, colleges can expect to see:

- decreased absenteeism

- decreased turnover

- greater employee satisfaction (measured by annual employee opinion or 360-degree feedback surveys)

- improved customer service

- longer average employee tenure

Teams Need Leaders, Too

Another key tenet of college admissions teamwork is leadership.

Leadership is crucial for creating successful collaboration cultures, particularly so in college admissions. That's because academic leaders know how to weave their goals, values, and ideals into the fabric of their academic institution.

Let's take a look at some key behaviors that campus leaders need to master to build a successful college admissions team.

Do we make teambuilding a priority? Leaders need to pay close attention to the progress of collaborative strategies in college admissions, particularly from team leaders.

Do we take the long view? Leaders need to stay ahead of and not react to incidents and organizational crises. That attention to detail will ensure that the college isn't sacrificing long-term goals for short-term fixes—fixes that could sabotage good teamwork efforts.

How do we delegate authority and dole out responsibilities? As I've already said, college leaders face unique challenges, especially given the shared governance culture that so dominates collegiate environs.

How do we recruit, select, promote, and replace? The politics involved in building an effective college admissions team can't be underestimated. Leaders must know how to communicate with their teams, how to motivate them, how to choose the right team members, and when it's time to let the underperforming team members move on down the road.

Of course, there's a lot more to team leadership than that, but the above tenets are crucial ones for collegiate leaders to absorb—and to execute.

Ties That Bind

From my position at TargetX, being a part of several unique teams that have helped schools revitalize and reinvigorate their college admissions programs has been a fascinating experience. Time and time again, working together as a multifunctioning unit, we laid the groundwork for establishing an ambitious strategic plan, achieved our plan's goals, and, perhaps most important, opened doors to opportunities otherwise not possible.

It's been quite a trip. Seeing a college's commitment to vision, mission, and controlled growth always seems to contribute to the confluence of energies that schools have created across their boundaries, those of both their physical campus and their global network of alumni, business partners, donors, and friends. Improving communication and cooperation between college admissions and fund-raising offices, for example, can increase a school's donor base. I've seen that result in significant gifts for capital improvements and scholarships.

Additionally, I've seen collaboration between a school's alumni and fund-raising offices result in increasing a school's presence in Europe, Asia, and the Middle East. As these examples demonstrate, collaboration opens doors that would otherwise remain closed.

One opportunity leads to another and another and still others, until the excitement and energy that are created become a driving institutional force. Once you've established a solid team, there really is no limit to the breadth and depth of what you can accomplish.

Chapter 6: The Team

Assuming you agree with the first five chapters that things are different now than they were in the past, how is your hiring practice changing?

❑ We hire individuals with experience in sales and/ or customer service.

❑ We hire individuals with more technical skills.

❑ We hire individuals able to understand and explain finances.

❑ We search beyond the institution (and alumni) for employees.

❑ We change compensation plans to accommodate different experience levels.

How comfortable are you as a leader in encouraging your team to embrace their mistakes?

❑ Very comfortable! There is usually an opportunity to turn it into something positive.

❑ I'm ok with it for the most part. We're all human, right?

❑ I'd rather not draw attention to it if I don't have to.

❑ Not at all. I just pretend it never happened and try to move on.

How well do you share information with your team (enrollment goals, budget details, financial aid plans, etc.)?

❑ I share everything (maybe too much).

❑ I share what I think is important.

❑ They're on a "need-to-know" basis—and they usually don't need to know.

❑ I don't think it's important for them to know this stuff.

Are you providing your recruiting team with the following tools and training:

❑ sales training

❑ financial aid training

❑ CRM system

❑ joint team calendars

❑ laptop

❑ smart phone

❑ internet access when out of the office

7

The Conversation

With Guest Author: Adrienne Bartlett

Don't chase the tools, chase the goals.
—Howard Kang, BlueFuego

While conversations still occur in person, with this generation in particular, many conversations take place online, a fact that might intimidate some admissions departments. (We'll focus on the importance of in-person conversations in chapter 8.)

I've spent plenty of time in this book talking about fear of change. Universities tend to be entrenched in a culture of control that has been challenged by new technology and a new generation born with tools that are counter to a single source of control.

But six chapters into this book, if there's one point I hope I've really driven home it's that change is a positive agent. Fear is a darkroom where only negatives can develop.

Perhaps nowhere is fear of change more rampant than in the use of the web for recruiting. It is the epitome of challenging a traditional "talk-at" style of marketing and replacing it with the new "talk with" methods. It's about control of the message, medium, and timing—and the demise of such control.

- According to the Pew Internet & American Life Project, 18–24-year-olds are the most likely to have a social network profile, with 75 percent having registered with at least one site. The numbers steadily trend downward from there, however, with 57 percent adoption among 25–34-year-olds and 30 percent among 45–54-year-olds, finishing with just 7 percent of Americans aged 65 and older on a social network.

- According to Pew Research's "Generations Online in 2009" study, Internet users aged 12–32 are more likely than older users to read other people's blogs and to write their own; they are also considerably more likely than older generations to use social networking sites and to create profiles on those sites. Teens in the Millennial generation are also significantly more likely than older generations to send instant messages to friends.

- According to Harris Interactive (and this is my favorite), 42 percent of teens participating in the study, "Teenagers: A Generation Unplugged" claim they can accurately text blindfolded.

I'm not surprised by these numbers. To kids, it only makes sense to connect with their peers online.

Unfortunately, I don't see that same enthusiasm for the social web among college admissions officers, and certainly not at the highest reaches of the college president's office. Not only do college officers mostly shun social networking tools, they fear opening themselves up to the authentic conversations that such tools, by their very essence, promote.

Time and time again, I hear the sad refrain "but what if someone says something bad about our school?" when I bring up the idea of a webcast or a blog or even a webpage with an interactive element.

That said, I'm not the one on the front lines of how schools are harnessing the power of the social web but there is someone on the team who is—TargetX's vice president for client experience, Adrienne Bartlett.

Adrienne works with our clients to educate them on current trends in admissions marketing and helps them develop more effective strategies for recruiting best-fit students. Adrienne is the creator of TargetX's popular "Free on Friday" webcast series, which she regularly contributes to in addition to her weekly XpertTips blog. When she's not working directly with clients, Adrienne is a popular speaker on the use of new media and the social web for recruitment.

That's why I'll be turning the rest of the chapter over to her. She can tell you best how colleges are achieving success by learning to give up control and embrace the online conversations surrounding their brand.

Guest Author: Adrienne Bartlett

Social Networking: The Big Picture

I don't always agree with Brian on everything (where's the fun in that?), but we do agree on the need for colleges to get over their fears and learn to use new technologies better in their recruitment efforts.

No doubt about it, many colleges are simply uncomfortable with the loss of control that comes with using social technologies.

Specifically, I think the things that bother schools most about online communication are the instability and newness of the medium.

Ironically, prospects don't tend to see it that way. For them, these tools and technologies have always been part of how they interact with the world—and they're expecting the same from the college search process. Make no mistake, the students attending your college are all members of the so-called Internet generation—they know this technology much better than you probably do. And that's a real fear of schools these days. As Brian has already said in this book, competition between colleges is only going to get more intense in the next few years. How do you continue to effectively market your school if you're also relinquishing some of the control over your message to the students themselves? And how do you foster social networking at your school without having it explode in your face?

Then there's the "fear" factor. No doubt, fear breeds resistance. There's a line of thinking that maybe social media isn't that important, worse, that it has the ability to hurt schools' recruiting efforts. Some professionals in the field have said that social networking technology has become a crutch for colleges' marketing departments. They've got their Facebook and Twitter accounts, sure, but they're not saying anything different with them. The packaging has changed but the message stays the same, in other words.

Way too often colleges lose out on great admissions candidates because they do not know how to communicate effectively with them. They aren't even familiar with the same tools that students use to communicate with each other.

Consequently, any "best practices" campaign must rely heavily on technology tools that students actually use, (like blogs, social networks, emails, and other communication tools that work best with today's students). College recruiters must learn how to reach out to students in the way that students are most comfortable and in a way appropriate for the medium, which means they need to understand that social tools

Social Networking on the Rise

The academic community isn't where it needs to be yet, but progress is being made on the social networking front.

Consider this study from the National Association for College Admission Counseling (NACAC) released in 2009. The study estimates that 25 percent of colleges surveyed indicated that they used web search or social networking technology to locate information about prospective students. The paper suggests that colleges are also more likely than not to use social media in promotion and student recruitment.

"Social media tools, like Facebook, Twitter and blogs, are key to communicating with this generation of students," stated Joyce Smith, NACAC CEO. "While still no substitute for face-to-face interaction, social media have opened lines of communication and inquiry for both students and institutions that were inconceivable only a decade ago."

Among the study's findings:

- More than half (53 percent) of colleges monitor social media for "buzz" about their institution.

- A majority of colleges maintain a presence in social media, as 33 percent of colleges maintain a blog, 29 maintain a presence on social networking websites, 27 percent maintain message- or bulletin-boards, 19 percent employ video blogging, and 14 percent issue podcasts. Thirty-nine percent of colleges reported using no social media technology.

- Eighty-eight percent of admissions offices believed social media were either "somewhat" or "very" important to their future recruitment efforts.

We're not exactly at critical mass—in fact, we're not even close—but, as we'll see, at least colleges and universities are beginning to recognize the "sky-is-the-limit" value of social networking.

shouldn't be treated as just another way to push out messages. When college recruiters learn how to participate and foster a dialogue, then the lines of conversation are opened—and the "marketing" campaign can begin.

Browsing for Buzz

The recent report from the National Association for College Admission Counseling, for example, found that one-fourth of colleges polled said they used the Web to find information about a recruit. More than half of them said they browsed social media sites for "buzz" about their schools, while 88 percent believed social media were somewhat to very important to their future recruitment efforts.

Social Networking Defined

Before we get into the ins and outs of using social tools to recruit students, it may be helpful to first consider that things are always changing. As a result, the ever-expanding world that we refer to as "the socal web" is not easy to peg down or describe in great detail.

Even as I write this, I'm well aware that much of what I'm saying could be outdated or considered "old news" by the time you read it. But the basics won't change—and the social web basics go beyond trends and fads and the latest, greatest tool. The basics are all about using technology to foster connections and conversations. And if you get that, then you're on the right track.

It seems like all the time now we hear about the latest trend sweeping the web—be it microblogging sites like Twitter to photo-sharing communities like Flickr. What they all have in common is that they are based on the same, simple premise: bringing people together.

For practical purposes, we'll eschew the more obscure social media niches to focus on the big boys that currently rule the web, namely Facebook and blogging sites (there are a bunch). Add to these other technology-driven communication tools and you begin to see that maintaining an online presence requires your college admissions department to juggle many responsibilities at the same time.

> ### Website Tip: Students Want Ease-of-Use
>
> A 2009 report from the education consulting firm Noel-Levitz called "Scrolling toward Enrollment," polled over one thousand high school seniors and found that while students believe colleges should maintain a social media presence, their main concern is being able to easily navigate the institution's website.

Let's start with Facebook, which took root on college campuses in the middle of the first decade of the twenty-first century as a kind of real-time, online yearbook. The idea, obviously, caught on quickly, such that now the site is one of the most widely heralded and valuable franchises on the web. It's a serious recruitment tool for colleges because it offers a comprehensive and multifaceted approach to communicating with students and connecting them with current students as well as each other.

Many schools are following their students' lead and setting up their own Facebook pages and groups. Other schools have decided to take that approach a step further and have integrated Facebook into their larger marketing strategy.

If that sounds a little excessive for what is ostensibly an online diversion for young people, well, get used to it. Social networking sites are not just the playgrounds of students anymore. They are proving to have applications in business, medicine, education—even government.

Watch Out for Social Networking Scams

When Brad J. Ward worked as the electronic communications coordinator for Butler University, he paid close attention to his school's presence on Facebook. One evening he noticed some suspicious activity while investigating a question from a colleague and decided he needed to warn the higher education community. So, true to form, Brad blogged about it.

What followed was a stream of scandal and intrigue rarely seen in higher education marketing. On his higher ed marketing blog, Andrew Careaga of Missouri University of Science and Technology deemed the scandal "Facebookgate"—and it was heavily covered by media across industries.

Here's the skinny: While digging deeper into a question from a colleague, Brad uncovered hundreds of Class of 2013 groups posing as official college and university groups on Facebook. He found that they were being created and/or maintained by the same group of people—none of whom were actually prospective students or applicants. He began posting about his findings, driving over 11,000 hits in twenty-four hours to his popular SquaredPeg.com blog.

Concerned about spam and questionable data-mining practices, Brad also began a Google Doc to try to tie the names of the schools together. Others were quick to join his effort. Eventually, they were able to trace the origin of the groups to a Pittsburgh-based company that publishes college guidebooks. The CEO of the firm confirmed his company's involvement but noted that they "cut ties" with all of the groups. That's too close a call for a college looking to put its best foot forward on Facebook. So let's share what I think are some key takeaways from the incident.

■ You can't hide from social media. And in this tumultuous environment, authenticity is king. If your efforts lack transparency, they will be exposed. Don't be afraid to be who you are and say that in your online efforts.

■ Protecting your prospects means paying attention to the online conversation surrounding your institution.

■ To successfully manage social media efforts (like maintaining a Facebook presence), someone has to be in charge—and that someone has to know what they're doing. In Butler's case, they were immediately on top of the issue because Brad Ward intuitively knew to dig deeper when things didn't add up. It's not just about policing for inappropriate content—it's about understanding the risks and benefits of the social web and proceeding accordingly.

■ Be careful whom you "friend"—as we've learned, on many sites, it's easy to pretend you're someone you're not.

Today you'll find Brad Ward using his acumen for all things "social" to help clients all over the world. He left Butler to begin BlueFuego, a firm that specializes in helping colleges develop and execute social recruitment strategies.

Demand for Technology: From Your Future Students

The fact is that there is a right and a wrong way to communicate online. Technology needs to be viewed as a component of successful recruiting—it's not a solution by itself. Blasting out humdrum mass emails and tweeting about irrelevant factoids aren't going to impress students—they're just going to make your college look like it's crashing a party. Worse, it makes your recruiting efforts seem inauthentic.

Let's go through some effective ways of using social media to reach out to potential students. Believe me, the market is out there. According to a recent Pew Internet & American Life Project survey, more than two-thirds of students maintain online social network profiles. Getting them to listen to your message is the real test of your recruiting mettle.

These are not just hopeful musings—there are real data to suggest that social media is not the ultimate solution to every college's marketing problems. A report by DemandEngine revealed that students would rather be contacted by college admission departments directly than through Twitter or Facebook. Clearly not everyone is enamored with the concept of college recruiters tweeting their way into students' lives.

Yes, it can be unpredictable as well as risky for colleges. But social networking is not just a new type of technology—at its core this trend is really about people's desire to connect with each other. And what's fundamental to any form of communication is that there is some risk involved of sounding out of touch and irrelevant. For the most part, the real problem with social networking and other forms of online communication is that colleges are just not using them effectively.

So how do you get started—or start improving—on your own social recruitment efforts?

One of the most important steps a school must take before planning a social strategy is to first research the tools you are interested in using. You can learn a great deal by using technology in your own life to learn the "rules of the road"

Let's lay out some more tips to maximize your social recruitment initiatives. (The objective is to familiarize yourself with the customs and lexicon that surround each medium you've chosen.)

■ Set up Google alerts to monitor mentions of your institution across the web.

■ Visit Technorati.com, a search engine that allows you to search through millions of blogs.

■ Set up your own, personal Facebook account to see how it works.

■ Listen to some podcasts—digital sound or video media files—on iTunes (you can download it off Apple's website if you don't already have it).

■ Look and listen—keep tabs on what other colleges are doing with their campaigns.

■ Ask yourself some key questions: What makes your college unique? What do you do best? What is your city or geographical region like? What are its selling points? The answers to these questions are the primary messages you want to convey to potential students.

■ Find out what students want. Actively engage in simple student questionnaires via email or a free service like surveymonkey.com.

Once you've done your research and have begun developing a social strategy for your school, take some concrete steps to ensure you've got your hands on the reins and are in control of the tools you're using and the messages your school is managing.

■ Create a sound social management policy. How is your social networking program going to augment your school's educational objectives? A clear, concise, and compelling policy can set the tone and terms for things like blogging policies, Facebook campaigns, and website chat room protocols.

■ Put someone who "gets it" in charge and then get out of his or her way. It's important to include others in your efforts, but you'll still need a leader who is well versed in both social tools and college recruiting. Finding the right person—and letting him or her lead—is 90 percent of the challenge.

- Create a good admissions blog. Get some word-of-mouth going on the benefits of going to your school. For a good example, I've always liked Ball State University's blog site: http://www.bsu.edu/reallife/.

- Organize your social campaigns. Like any college admissions outreach endeavor, social networks need to be nurtured and managed. That requires a great deal of testing, delegation, scheduling, and even more testing. For a good look at how you can put your social networking hub all in one place, see the University of California's Haas School of Business social networking portal at http://www.haas.berkeley.edu/haas/about/socialmedia/index.html.

When you do want to interject an official college voice into this community, try to be as helpful and informative as you can. Don't waste students' time—give them the content they want. Lists are a popular feature, for example—you can use your social networking tools to post features like "The 10 Things to Do Before You Graduate," "The 10 Best Campus Eateries," or "The 10 Best Studying Spots on Campus." These lists are not only a fun way to get students talking about their college—you can utilize poll software or web tools like Survey Monkey to let them submit their own answers—but also provide a glimpse of collegiate life to potential applicants. Web forums are also a useful tool to get students talking about your college—invite them to post under topics such as "What's on your mind as you enter college?" or "What made you become interested in this college?" You can even use social networking to get your current students talking with your potential ones—set up a rotating text box or forum post, for example, that allows recruits to ask questions about life at your college. Trust me, they'd much rather get this information from their peers than from your official marketing campaign.

Another advantage of social media is that it allows your college to create a community for applicants before they even set foot on your campus. Many businesses are starting to create applications specially designed to allow colleges to establish meaningful connections with recruits through social networking sites, for example. They bridge the gap between colleges and students through the use of online communication technology.

Above all, keep working on it. After all, the biggest risk is taking no risk at all. Go into the process knowing that you're on the right track and that by using social networking you're connecting with kids on the playing field of their choice.

Consider this quote from Eric Mattson, CEO of Financial Insite, Inc., a Seattle-based research firm, and a key contributor to a Society for New Communication Research Study:

> Those graduating high school today have been exposed to the Internet since childhood. They are constantly connected—plugged into digital music

devices, cell phones, the Internet, instant messenger and social networks, perhaps all on the same device. This world of interactivity and hyper-communication has fundamentally changed how teenagers and young adults receive, process, and act on information.

Social media have undeniably changed the landscape of college admissions. The value of these social media tools for college admissions offices cannot be underestimated. As more and more young people spend increased amounts of time communicating online, an institutional presence will become mandatory.

Building a Better Admissions Process, Blog by Blog

Blogging, too, is an effective way to interact with students. Condensed from "web log," a blog is simply an online journal. Like most other social media, blogs started out as a way for ordinary people to personalize their web experience. Blogging capitalized on the egalitarian spirit of the web by allowing just about anybody to share his or her opinions and stories with audiences from all over the world.

Many colleges now employ students part-time to write blogs about college life. These student blogs are useful not only to students already attending that school, but also to high school students who want to get a "real" take on college life. In some cases, student blogs have developed into serious news sources—at MIT, for example, student blogs were deeply involved in the reporting of a scandal that caused the school's dean of admissions to resign a few years ago. While that's not always conducive to college administrators' interests in controlling their message, it does give blogging a legitimacy that registers with students.

The controversies surrounding blogging serve as a good launching point into the debate over social media on college campuses. Don't be mistaken—just because college administrators may realize that social networking is important doesn't mean that they all trust it. I'm sure you have questioned at some point the benefit of getting involved in technology that is student-oriented and student-controlled. And to be honest, there are some disadvantages to social networking.

Five Tips for Building Your Best Blogging Community

Building a blog is one thing: getting good bloggers is quite another. Consider these keys when recruiting the talent needed for your school's blogging campaign.

1. **Represent (your student body)** Whether you're a huge state school or a small commuter campus or have a super-diverse city environment make sure the bloggers you choose represent the true makeup of your student body.

2. **Look beyond your office** Don't just hire the "good kids" (i.e. your student ambassadors). Many of them are over-involved already and may not be able to dedicate the time necessary to post. Plus they don't always "represent" (see above tip).

3. **Mix up the media** Hire for personality and storytelling ability—then play to their strengths. Not all bloggers have to write. In fact, only the good writers should write. Have a blogger with a larger-than-life personality? Let them do video posts. Know a budding photographer? Give him a photo blog. If you utilize their talents, they'll be more into it and more likely to post regularly.

4. **It's not "all about the Benjamins."** Incentives don't always have to be monetary. Consider letting bloggers move in early, register for classes first, have dinner with the president once a semester, and so forth. The more you make them feel appreciated and special, the more likely they are to stay involved and go the extra mile.

5. **Get directions** Encourage bloggers to find a clear direction or voice for their blog. Think about having film majors do movie reviews or fashion majors post pictures of their outfits or assignments each week. English majors can relate the books they're reading in class to campus life and new freshmen can relate the ups and downs of their transition to college. Great blogs are focused—remember you can't be all things to all people.

Blogging the MIT Way

A recent article in the *New York Times* titled "M.I.T. Taking Student Blogs to the Nth Degree" demonstrates that the Massachusetts Institute of Technology—unsurprisingly, given the bright minds that inhabit the school—"get it" when it comes to student blogs.

Here are some key points from the article:

■ They don't censor or edit student posts.

■ They hold a writing contest to hire new bloggers.

■ They primarily look for involved students who are good communicators.

■ They allow comments.

■ Posts appear on the main admissions homepage.

■ They've fostered in-person connections by hosting a "Meet the Bloggers" event.

■ They choose a sampling of writers with "different majors, ethnicities, residence halls and, particularly, writing styles."

The Authenticity Theme

What you'll probably notice about all of these different technologies is that they get back to the key term we've been discussing throughout this book: authenticity.

While it's true that, as I said before, many businesses are getting in on the act, a large percentage of social networking activity still takes place between ordinary people, especially students. Go on YouTube, for example, and see some of the college-themed videos there. You will find thousands of videos of students just goofing around for their friends. They're not getting paid to do any of this, and that's the point—these sites are about interacting in a community.

You can understand then why some students would balk at having this community become the next scene for high-stakes college recruiting. And it's why some schools' social networking efforts fail. They're inauthentic—they're not hiding the fact that all those tweets and Facebook postings and other cool online tricks are just fancier versions of the impersonal, bottom line–driven recruiting tactics that students had sought to avoid in the first place. Websites like "College Confidential" (http://www.collegeconfidential.com/) and "Rate My Professor" (http://www.ratemyprofessors.com/), for instance, embrace the idea that students go online to avoid that marketing hype and get the unvarnished truth about their schools, which aren't supposed to be looking.

That brings us to a critical point about online communication: You need to abandon the notion that your school will have 100 percent control over its message on the web. And you need to accept that this is okay. The new rules of social marketing say that top-down advertising—pushing a message onto your customers—doesn't work, because there is not a captive audience on the web. Instead, content sharing has created a model where word of mouth builds a product's reputation from the ground up—it's viral marketing, in other words. Colleges can use this scenario to their advantage.

Take student blogging, for instance. Many schools are tempted to recruit their best and brightest to post ringing endorsements of their school. They'll even pay some students for their efforts. The result, unfortunately, is not always very authentic. Instead, why not look beyond your student ambassadors to find some of the students who don't always show up on the administration's radar? These students have a variety of interests—they don't even have to be writers, as photoblogs and other media are also very popular online. Give them a little guidance on blog themes and subject matter, but allow them to have independent voices, too. And don't assume that money is the only incentive. Try to make bloggers feel like they're the stars of your social networking campaign. Chances are, if you treat them right and effectively promote their work, they'll be great assets for your school's recruiting efforts.

As Brian has said throughout this book, one of your main goals as a college admissions department needs to be telling your college's story authentically to students. Social tools are incredibly useful toward this end, because they are media fundamentally based on the idea of unfiltered, authentic communication. Don't make your online communication strategy about your college—make it about the students. Let them tell your story for you, warts and all.

The Takeaway

The real advantages of social recruiting are easy to see even in the simplest forays into using new technologies.

In fact, part of the beauty of the social web is the ease with which you can try something new. If it works, great; if not, just take it down and try something else. The medium is incredibly flexible, and you should always be on the lookout for new trends that will help you broaden your reach. Social networking is relatively cheap—aside from some of the more specific software and applications on the market, most of the technology out there today is free and available on websites.

Facebook Nation

It's no surprise that colleges are looking to Facebook, the world's most trafficked social network, for recruitment and outreach. According to a recent Pew Internet & American Life Project study, 68 percent of full-time students and 71 percent of part-time students maintain social networking profiles. Additionally, another study conducted by the Center for Marketing Research at the University of Massachusetts Dartmouth found that 61 percent of college admissions offices use social networks to recruit students.

So don't get too caught up in the strategic planning and cost-benefit analysis on this one. Strategy and planning are all well and good, but at a certain point they can paralyze you from actually doing something. Also keep in mind that social media is not a "catchall" solution to every recruitment marketing woe. It's just another piece of the puzzle—albeit an incredibly timely, relevant, and important piece.

Social networking and online communication can seem like the final frontier of marketing at times—it requires a leap of faith. But to truly be able to market your school effectively, you need to go to where your market is instead of waiting around for your market to find you. And if there's one thing we know for certain, it's that social networking is a trend that is not going to subside anytime soon. Sure, maybe the technology will change, but the goal of bringing people together will remain. And as a college admissions department representative, that's what your job is all about.

The Future Is Now

Despite the initial reluctance of colleges and universities to embrace the social nature of the web, we're finally starting to see some progress.

I recently saw a University of Massachusetts study that says use of social networking tools is on the rise in college admissions offices. The study—"Social Media and College Admissions: Researcher Presents Findings on How Colleges Use Social Media to Recruit and Screen Prospective Students"—shows that there was a 32 percent increase in the use of social networking applications by college admissions offices between 2007 and 2008. The report, which is based on the first statistically significant longitudinal study on the use of social media in college admissions, demonstrates the rapid pace and expanding breadth at which colleges are adopting social media technology to both recruit and research prospective students.

The UMass study of five hundred admissions officers at U.S. four-year colleges and universities, is an unusually interesting one. The researchers discovered that college admissions officers are actually outpacing the corporate sector in the use of social media with just 15 percent of college admissions offices reporting that they do not use any social media. In 2007, 39 percent said they didn't use social media.

In that time period, the UMass study discovered year-to-year increases across the board in social networking, including the number of college admissions offices that say they use the following applications:

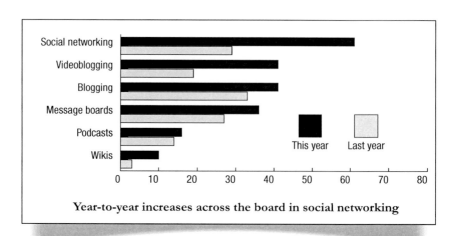

Year-to-year increases across the board in social networking

Brian's Interjection:

I'm asked frequently what I think comes after web 2.0. I joke that I believe that in a web 3.0 world we'll realize we've all shared way too much and we'll scurry away to our own separate corners of the world. Funny yes, but I hope I'm not correct.

But I'd have to agree with the study's conclusion that there is plenty of work to be done before the college recruiting industry really hits high gear. Admissions departments are still heavily print-focused in their communication strategy, staffing priorities, and budget allocations.

"There is evidence of enthusiasm and eagerness to embrace these new communications tools, but there is also evidence that these powerful tools are not being utilized to their potential," says the UMass study. "Schools using social media must learn the 'rules of engagement' in the online world in order to maximize their effectiveness."

I believe that's the main takeaway on the issue of social recruitment in college admissions. While colleges are definitely engaging in digital outreach, it's all too easy to get caught up in the tools and miss the real point—that it's really all about conversation.

To sum things up I go back to the quote I chose to begin this chapter. When it comes to online communication with prospects, "Don't chase the tools, chase the goals."

Chapter 7: The Conversation

Search online for mention of your school on the following websites:

❑ Google.com   ❑ Technorati.com

❑ YouTube.com   ❑ CollegeConfidential.com

❑ Facebook.com   ❑ search.Twitter.com

❑ Delicious.com

❑ Setup Google Alerts for mentions of your institution or specific programs. Learn more by visiting www.google.com/alerts.

To be effective, a social web strategy has to be "sustainable." Ask yourself the following questions to be sure your plan is on track for long-term success:

Have you chosen online initiatives that relate to specific enrollment goals?

Initiative: _____Goal: _____

Initiative: _____Goal: _____

Initiative: _____Goal: _____

Initiative: _____Goal: _____

How will you measure success?

_____

_____

_____

Who owns (a.k.a. manages) your social web efforts?

_____

Have you given them the tools, time, and resources to succeed? ❑ Yes ❑ No

8

The Visit

With Guest Author: Jeff Kallay

The Experience is *the Marketing!*
—Joe Pine and Jim Gilmore

On a crisp autumn day in western New York, something revolutionary happened in college admissions.

Dr. Charles M. Edmonson, president of Alfred University, piloted the inaugural run of the university's seven-passenger admissions conference bike.

Trust me. You have to see a conference bike to believe it and you have to ride it to really appreciate it. Measuring 8' x 6' x 4', the conference bike has three wheels, weighs four hundred pounds, and features a pedaling mechanism that allows all passengers to sit in the round—literally in a "conference" setup—and pedal forward regardless of their position on the bike. The driver faces forward, and he or she navigates and brakes.

To the fanfare of the Alfred students, faculty, staff, guests, and various members of the media, President Edmonson, sat in the driver's seat and rode the bike along with six Alfred Ambassadors, all pedaling while Edmonson steered through the ceremonial ribbon. Soon after, various members of the community took rides on the bike, and later that day, a prospective family conducted part of their Alfred campus visit and tour on the conference bike. Other prospective families would do the same on special tours offered on Mondays and Fridays. Those who climb the cycle are given a special "Toured Hard" athletic gray T-shirt with the Alfred Admissions Bike screen printed on the back and sign a special log to commemorate their run on the bike.

The conference bike is unique and authentic to Alfred University. And it's a good lesson for colleges looking to spruce up or even go back to the drawing board to fix their broken campus visit programs.

That's what Alfred did. Alfred's decision to incorporate a seven-passenger bike tour option into their campus visit program was several semesters in the making. They acknowledged how important the campus visit is, they fixed their basics (making countless improvements), and they implemented experiential improvements and ideas and then added a conference bike into the mix.

And that's the action plan we'll take you through in this chapter. Actually, I'm designating a "tour guide" of my own to walk you through this chapter—TargetX's own vice president of consulting, Jeff Kallay. Jeff has made his passion his career—helping colleges and universities stage more authentic and memorable visit experiences for prospective students and their families.

You couldn't be in better hands.

Guest Author: Jeff Kallay

As any of the college admissions officers I know can attest, I have lots to say about staging the optimal college visit experience. But we could use some background first, before we get into the *actionable* items.

First, let's realize how important the campus visit is to students and their families. We all know it, but the research proves it.

- Seventy-one percent of high school students say that the campus visit is the most trusted source of information (2007 Eduventures research).

- Campus visit programs rank in the top five most effective of fifty-three overall recruitment tactics at four-year public and private schools (2009 Noel-Levitz).

- The campus visit is the top influencer in a student's decision to apply and enroll (2005 Art & Science StudentPoll).

- Ninety percent of students tell us: "I visited campus and it just felt right."

The "we" I referred to above is the TargetX Campus Visit Experience Team, led by TargetX's chief experience officer, Trent Gilbert.

Our Experience Team is a unique group of experience economy experts dedicated to helping colleges and universities host authentic, memorable, and engaging campus visits. The idea and business plan were hatched by Trent Gilbert and me in 2006. I was developing new business at a firm in Atlanta and Trent was running the ambassadors and events programs in the admissions office at Elon University. We brought the idea to Brian Niles's office and TargetX started a service dedicated to helping schools rethink their all-important campus visit. Hundreds of clients and countless campus tours later, our campus visit consulting service is improving the prospective family experience one campus at a time as it expands in staff, number of clients, and offerings. Throughout the rest of this chapter, I will share our expertise, experience, and wisdom with you.

Rethinking the Campus Visit

While Alfred University is a client, and we did recommend the conference bike, it wasn't just a random attempt at creativity. We weren't being creative for the sake of being creative.

More specifically, they didn't just run out and buy a seven-passenger bike thinking that the idea was so novel that students would choose to attend their college because of it. Alfred's decision to buy their conference bike was the result of a commitment to the overall campus visit program and was based on other successful ideas and changes throughout the years. (We'll talk about the details of Alfred University's campus visit in a case study toward the end of this chapter.)

That brings me to the governing principle we want to make about staging a campus visit and about any recruitment idea. As I said, it's not about being clever for the sake of being clever.

Let's look at some key themes.

The "creativity" conundrum In this rough-and-tumble economy, it certainly wasn't about doing more with less as is the campus visit format these days. The "Club Med" mentality of higher education during the last decade brought on an amenities arms race that trickled down to recruitment strategies and tactics. Even with the sluggish economy, it's still impacting the campus visit. Schools think that there is some magical "E Ticket" campus visit idea or experience (for those of you old enough to remember Disney parks ranked rides with tickets) that will convince marginal students to enroll. There is no magic formula when it comes to staging a campus visit. But there is hard work, a strategic plan, a commitment of funds, staff, and, resources, and, most important, rendering authentic experiences.

Rendering authenticity It's a notion posed in the 2008 Harvard Business School book *Authenticity: What Consumers Really Want*, written by our friends Joe Pine and Jim Gilmore (they also wrote *The Experience Economy: Work Is Theater and Every Business a Stage*). We've dedicated an entire chapter to the idea of authenticity, and it's even more important focus on authenticity so when it comes to the campus visit.

The Grass Really is Greener...

This is a point worth delving into, so let's talk about the grass on your campus.

There are some basics that you need to address and these are often the most frequently overlooked by our campus visit clients. Often clients hire us expecting "big ideas" to improve their visits, yet they don't yet have the basics (including landscaping) covered.

Authenticity is being comfortable in your own *institutional* skin and revealing it to your prospective students so they can decide for themselves. Great campus visits connect with more *best-fit* and *right-fit* students. The president of one of our campus visit clients asked our experience team, "What is the biggest mistake we can make with the campus visit?" Our reply, "To have a family get in the car after visiting and say, 'It's a nice school but I don't fully understand it.'" Meaning to not render authenticity. The biggest mistake is to confuse visitors about who you are as an institution.

Brands are mirrors and college is an intimate product choice The right choice is the best fit. It's our responsibility to help students find their *best-fit* school. That's why a campus visit should render authentically that which is real about your school. Not just your best facilities, programs, and students. It should show visitors all sides of your school. Millennials are savvy; they crave the genuine article. While their helicopter parents might be caught up in amenities, we find most students take ownership of the campus as is. And, often, the seemingly random place or space on campus becomes their favorite. Millennials want a campus visit that shows the real *you*. They know the grass isn't always green and the sun doesn't always shine.

Campus Visit Boot Camp

In academia, as in real life, there's theory and there's execution.

Let's move on and address the actual physical steps needed to improve your campus visit, the Top Ten Basics, including logistics and setting that make a campus visit run smoothly.

1. **Website and information** Go to your school's website and put yourself in the mind-set of a prospective parent or student. Try to find the Visit information. How many clicks is it? It shouldn't be more than two. Once you find it, does it clearly and concisely explain visit options, and how to register, and does it manage the expectations?

2. **Managing the expectations** Do your campus visit brochures, websites, and confirmation materials clearly explain details like amount of time on campus, how that time will be distributed (information session, walking tour, interview, lunch, etc.), where to park, where to start the visit, and options beyond the group visit? It should.

3. **Confirmation materials** We're shocked at the number of schools that don't send out emails or regular mail confirmation materials (let alone make confirmation calls the day before). No doubt about it, families are going to forget these when they go on their road trip so make maps, phone numbers, and other details readily available on your website, and at local hotels, and consider having a visit hotline for them to call.

4. **Erecting signage to campus** When a family is coming from the airport or driving on the highway, how well does the *wayfinding* signage direct them to your campus? Again, we're shocked at how poorly most schools handle the basic component of a quality experience. Work with your state, county, and local municipalities to ensure that you have it right. Above all, don't try to route families some complicated way because you think that has the best curb appeal.

5. **Wayfinding signage once on campus** Get in your car and drive to your campus as if it were the first time and not as somebody who has been driving to campus for the past several years. If you were a parent driving, where would you go? How is your signage to parking and to the starting point of the campus visit? Nobody likes to be lost or late, and improper or lack of proper wayfinding confuses guests, adds to their stress level, and starts the visit on a negative note. Admissions is your revenue source; it most likely generates the most amount of visitors to campus on a daily basis, so you need to get those guests to their visit start in an efficient manner. The main takeaway: admissions should have visibly larger and more wayfinding.

6. **Parking** You can't have enough visitor parking near your admissions office visitor center—and it needs to be free. Even if you're running a state school, charging guests for parking is an insult. It's not hospitable. Families are spending thousands of dollars to go on college road trips, and the last thing they want is to pay for parking. Also, the parking spaces should be clearly marked for *Prospective Students* or *Admissions Guests*, and not just generic *Visitor* signage. Make sure these spaces are policed and protected. Two of our clients do this well. The first is Winthrop University, a public school in Rockhill, South Carolina. They had a problem with students, faculty, and staff parking in admissions spaces. So they incorporated parking lot greeters, students who stand out in the parking lot about thirty minutes before tours begin. They "protect" the spaces from non-visitors, greet families, give them their parking pass, and direct them to their destination. It's authentic to the warm southern hospitality at Winthrop and protects the spaces. The other is Lake Erie College, a small private school in Ohio. The campus safety

squad didn't have the resources to protect admissions spaces so they made the campus visit director a safety officer. She is able to ticket those who park in the admissions spaces. Be creative.

7. **Admissions spaces and welcome centers** These locations give prospective students and their parents their first impressions. They should be comfortable, clean, roomy and authentic in look and feel. Invest in your admissions space like Dr. David Pollick, president of Birmingham-Southern College, did. There, admissions used to be in the basement of the administration building, not symbolic of a top-tier national liberal arts college, nor did it match the rest of the campus quality. He designed and built one of the best admissions offices right by the main entrance to campus. It's beautiful, but it's functional and is a point of pride for the college and connects with prospective families.

8. **Bathrooms** Invariably, the first question guests ask when they arrive is, "Where are your restrooms?" Too often, most of our clients are embarrassed to answer. These are guests to your campus, much like guests to your home. They should be directed to a quality facility. Angered by the sad state of admissions bathrooms, our chief experience officer (CXO), Trent Gilbert, sponsored the TargetX Bowl: the search for the best admissions guest bathrooms. We were proud to give awards to our clients Birmingham-Southern and the University of Delaware (best small college and large university, respectively). We also received countless emails from admissions staffers saying they would have entered if it had been a worst bathroom contest. Your admissions staff shouldn't be ashamed or embarrassed of facilities at your school. Fix them up. Make them glisten. And remember, admissions areas are always the exception. They need extra housekeeping and extra maintenance budgeted because of their daily footprint.

9. **Landscaping** Dads and moms are DIY experts. If you can't mow your lawns, trim your shrubs and bushes, edge, de-ice, or repair your sidewalks, how can you manage four years of a child's life and demand tens of thousands of dollars from a family? Consequently, don't cut back on landscaping. While some schools now rival Disney parks for their flora, we're just happy to see well-maintained and properly landscaped campuses. Susquehanna University does this well, and so should you.

10. **Campus buy-in** While the other basics are tangible, it's your job as a leader on campus to encourage campus buy-in of the campus visit. I've said many times that "it takes a campus to stage a campus visit." It's not just admissions' job. The parking deck cashier, dining hall attendant, department secretary, residence life staffer, and faculty all make an impression and render the nature of your campus to visitors. One of the best ways to get campus buy-in is to daily promote the campus visit and/or visitors via your school's daily internal email.

These basics seem so simple, but our experience team has captured thousands of photos that show that most schools miss them. Before you think about buying a conference bike, incorporating an "E Ticket" idea, or even hiring us, cover your basics.

Take a Test Run

Every semester your school's president, the vice president who leads facilities and housekeeping, and admissions staffers should take an official tour and audit your campus's visit and route. We're shocked by the number of times people on campus in charge of making a campus visit better never tour it. Often, the last time they toured was when they interviewed.

Key Steps in Mastering the Campus Visit

You've acknowledged how important the campus visit is, and you've begun to work on improving the basics. Now you can begin brainstorming authentic experiential ideas. Again, we emphasize that they have to be authentic. What works at one school doesn't work at another. Remember, Millennials don't value clever, they value what's real.

Ten Steps toward Staging a Better Campus Visit Experience

1. **Experiential** Is your school staging a *tour* or an *experience*? Here's a guide to filter yours.

Tour	Experience
One size fits all	Customized and personalized
Full of stats	Tells stories
Looks at buildings	Invites guests to engage in buildings
Tries to be all things to all people	Connects with "best-fit" students
Shows "campus only"	Shows where students really spend time
Settles for a messy campus	Prioritizes aesthetics
A long march	A memorable walk
Same as everyone else	Unique and distinctive
Involves only admissions	Involves entire campus

2. **Integrate the four E's** According to our friends Pine and Gilmore, all experiences we *experience* fit into one of these four E's: *Esthetic, Escape, Entertainment,* and *Education.* That's esthetics as in a sense of place. The first key to staging a sense of place is to ensure that you've got the aesthetics covered; this is why the basics are so important.

    Most campus visits are guilty of overemphasizing esthetics. A common refrain is "Hey, look at our buildings and facilities!" But a campus isn't that tangible. It's the intangibles that make up the campus community. Esthetics and entertainment are passive. The goal is to stage more authentic, memorable, and engaging campus visits that connect with more *best-fit* students.

    Consequently, the challenge is to create parts of the visit and tour that are more engaging and immersive. This leads to staging tours and visits that include more educational and escape components.

3. **Set the expectation** Nobody likes being lost. You need to put maps in your admissions office, in your information session, and in the hands of guests. And use them. Train guides to set the expectation of the route before walking, to show where they are going to go and where they can visit after the main tour. Use maps to reorient guests during the tour so they can get their bearings.

4. **Address your cues** In the experience economy, there are negative, positive, and missed cues. Most schools are guilty of having too many negative or missed cues. Negative cues are things like ill-kept facilities and lackluster landscaping. Missed cues are bit more elusive. They're often the seemingly small things that truly reveal your campus: bulletin boards, outdoor spaces where students gather, or random places that, while not your newest or sexiest, are significant to your student experience.

5. **Customization** We all want what we want when we want it. Starbucks makes it "your drink;" iPods make their owner the DJ, listening to what they want; DVRs allow us to time shift and watch when we want. The same is true for tours and visits. Sure, families will want to see academic areas of interest, residential life and dining, and recreation facilities. But you've got to allow for customization after the main tour. Enable families to discover your campus based on their interests.

6. **Engage all the senses** Eighty-three percent of all marketing appeals to sight, and this is true for most campus tours. Much like concentrating on buildings, many schools make the same mistake when it comes to sensory engagement. We've got five senses but campus tours only concentrate on sight and sound—meaning we parade families around and talk-at them. Great tours and student tour guides

know how to engage all the senses. They sit families down and engage what we call the "sense of the butt." They stop and encourage you to smell or they invite you to touch and feel.

7. **Have a signature moment** Visitors to Rome often throw a coin in the Trevi Fountain. That's a signature moment. Chances are you've got countless signature moments throughout your tour route and they should be integrated into the tour. At California Lutheran University, prospective students have their photo taken with the "Enormous Luther" (a.k.a. Gumby) statue. Pace University's New York campus tours sit down in the theater where *Inside the Actor's Studio* is filmed. Signature moments don't have to be *enormous;* they just have to be real and authentic.

8. **Mix in the memorabilia** There are millions of Mickey Mouse ears reminding people of their visit to Disney parks. A college diploma is the ultimate memorabilia to remind graduates of their time on campus. Give guests campus memorabilia to remind them of your campus. Again, it should be unique and authentic. T-shirts are great, but they're redundant. Ohio State gives every guest a chocolate and peanut butter Buckeye. Very authentic.

9. **Tell stories (and statistics)** Stories are how most of us learn. But most campus tours are offensively, overwhelmingly about stats. Perhaps it's the nature of rankings and their influence over us all that tours are just treated as a dumping ground for bragging points and points of pride. But families don't remember stats. Nobody gets in the car after a campus visit and says, "13–1 student-teacher ratio— sign me up!" They'll remember stories about how the tour guide texted a professor at midnight regarding a question on a paper and that faculty member responded. Or, how a faculty member got her a referral for an internship. Stories keep it real.

While stats are important, it's even more important how you reveal them to your prospective families and who reveals them. Make sure admissions and student guides are saying the same thing.

Admissions staff should present the stats (in an abbreviated time frame, not a one-hour information session) and student tour guides should tell stories that reveal the real nature and nomenclature of your campus. The authentic student experience.

That's why we've developed this to help you get in sync:

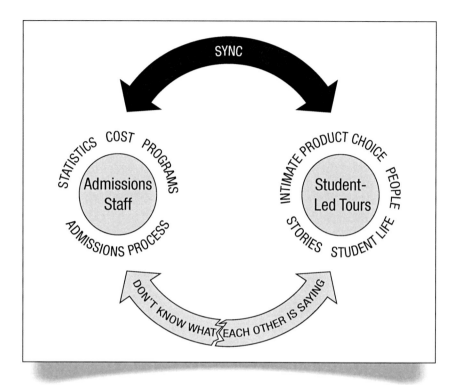

10. **Keep it real** We have to repeat it again: it's about staging a campus visit that is real and authentic, one that connects with best-fit students and doesn't connect with those for whom your school isn't a good fit.

The Hendrix Visit

That brings us to what we consider one of the best campus visits in higher education. It's been written about in the *New York Times* and *Chronicle of Higher Education* and is becoming the de facto standard: Hendrix College in Conway, Arkansas.

Hendrix College is known for their campus visit, which they call the "Hendrix Experience." They say if you don't know who Jimi Hendrix was or what the Hendrix Experience is, Hendrix College might not be the place for you.

Hendrix is a top-tier national liberal arts school that has always achieved, but its location has always been an issue. How do you convince people that great thinking has no borders? Hendrix always recruited the best and brightest in the state and in surrounding states, but it has had a limited national student body .

To grow beyond the state border, the leadership at Hendrix decided it wanted a more highly qualified and more nationally diverse student body. And it created a prospective student experience to help it get there. First, Hendrix did a year of planning regarding their campus visit. They read all the books on the experience economy and experiential marketing.

Then they reappropriated budgets and staff, taking a full-time senior associate position and making it a non-traveling coordinator of campus visits.

The next step was finding the budget to pay for it. They looked long and hard at high school travel, college fairs, and publications. They cut their print publications by 40 percent and travel by 30 percent. The funds were transferred toward prospective student experiences.

A defining notion was that it was smarter to invest in prospective students committed to traveling to campus.

Hendrix then took a negative cue of geography and turned it into a positive cue. Its biggest competitor is 3.5 hours away, so Hendrix crafted a customized experience that lasts most of the day. Their philosophy is that college is a big decision and Hendrix is a unique place that deserves a day; if you can't invest in a day, don't come tour.

It takes confidence to say no.

Hendrix stages a customized visit that integrates much of what you read in the preceding pages. Each prospective student attends class, meets one-on-one with faculty, walks the campus, eats lunch in the dining hall and drives away with a host of memorabilia. More important, they filter the visit through strong authenticity filters. Each idea isn't judged for being creative or clever but whether or not it is authentic to the Hendrix experience.

Hendrix is a unique place. In the deep South, it has no Greek community and for the past fifty years has had no football team. It's a place where geeks are celebrated and the passion and pursuit of the mind is the overarching part of the student experience.

Hendrix reveals this to prospective students.

And it's working well. Very well.

Since implementing and committing to the campus visit, Hendrix has been on a roll. Each freshman class has been larger than the class before and has possessed higher grade point averages and test scores. In fact, the average ACT of this incoming class was 30.

While Hendrix never recruited a class of more than 50 percent from out of state, 62 percent of the current freshman class is from out of state, and cross apps are now more national and include higher-ranked schools.

And while rankings don't matter, there's one category in which Hendrix was recently ranked #1 according to *U.S. News and World Report*: "Up and Coming National Liberal Arts Colleges."

In fact, six of the ten in this category are TargetX campus visit consult clients.

The other "Up and Coming" rankings were populated by a number of our campus visit clients as well.

Sure, we'd like to take credit for it, but we think that clients who are ready to overthrow dead culture know how important the campus visit is and they invest accordingly. Most are doing a great job of conveying an authentic version of their school to prospective families. They are connecting with more best-fit students and realize that a well-executed campus visit is key to reaching enrollment goals.

Overthrowing dead culture means not staging the same old same old campus visit. But it also means not being clever for the sake of clever.

Back to Alfred

To conclude, let's revisit Alfred University and their conference bike. To some it might seem that a seven-passenger bike as part of the tour is clever. But you need to know the entire story behind it.

Alfred had a decent campus visit before they brought us to campus to work with them. But the ambassadors weren't really engaged. They behaved more like student workers. Giving tours was just a job, not a passion. And the tour was a death march along the side of their mountain campus, but it didn't show all of campus, nor did it show the village of Alfred, which is really an extension of student life.

So Alfred's vice president of enrollment, Wendy Beckmeyer, empowered Jodi Bailey, director of marketing, and John Lewis, assistant director of admissions, to own the campus visit. They divided and conquered. John led the troops and Jodi took on campus. They took our report and cleaned up the basics. And they recruited students who really wanted to give tours and have fun.

One of the biggest investments was to buy a passenger van. Once families walked the nearly half mile out, the van would pick them up and drive them to the fitness center, through the village, and back up the mountain to admissions. One student came up with the graphics and another with a nickname for it.

Evaluations began improving. Families said that they saw more of campus and really appreciated the ride as the second part of the tour. Slowly the students started having more fun and telling more stories about what makes Alfred unique.

After three semesters of improvements and enhancements, we were back on campus for another meeting and tour guide training. During the training, we brainstormed with students and asked, "If time and money weren't barriers, what would you do to improve the campus visit?" A host of ideas came up that were forged into actual working ideas.

One student said, "Bikes are really big on our campus; we should offer a bike tour as an option." So we showed them the conference bike video and they all thought it was representative of Alfred. "We sit around up here in the mountains and talk." "Alfred's all about testing new things and meeting new people." "We want you to get outside of your comfort zone." "If you don't want to ride the bike and chat with others, you might not be a good fit for Alfred."

So the "wheels" were put into motion and within two months of the idea, Alfred launched the conference bike tour option on busy Mondays and Fridays. Prospective families reserve in advance and it's part of their visit along with a walking tour. Should there be an empty seat, current students and faculty and staff are encouraged to hop in and join the tour. And they do.

Will a conference bike convince a student to enroll? No. Does it help Alfred University render authenticity and capture the essence of the community at Alfred? Yes!

And it's fun. After all, college is fun. Your campus tour should be as well.

Chapter 8: The Visit

Take an "official" campus tour once a year.

❑ Register for your visit online or over the phone.

❑ Drive to and park on campus following directions provided.

❑ Take an official campus tour (preferably with a prospective student and family).

What grade would you give your entire campus visit experience? _____

How are the following components of your campus visit supporting your enrollment goals?

Your admissions messaging and student messaging:

_____

_____

Your admissions/visitor space:

_____

_____

Your overall campus aesthetics:

_____

_____

If time or money were no object, how would you improve the campus visit?

_____

_____

_____

9

The Economy

With Guest Authors: Jim Scannell and Kathy Kurz

Never let a good crisis go to waste.
—Rahm Emanuel

Let's keep the *expert* theme going here in chapter 9, where I'll let two of our friends weigh in on the number one issue on the minds of college administrators: how will the crumbling economy impact my school and my school's admissions program?

Our chapter experts this go-round are Jim Scannell and Kathy Kurz, the chief principals at Scannell & Kurz, Inc., a provider of higher education consulting services that has worked with over 250 academic institutions on more than 350 projects.

Jim's special area of expertise falls in recruitment—from mentoring admissions leaders to building new demand through data analysis and the development of strategic communications. Jim's administrative career has spanned over twenty-five years of leadership in admissions, financial aid, and enrollment management at Boston College, Cornell University, and the University of Rochester. In addition, Jim has authored numerous publications on enrollment management including *On Choosing a College That Is Right for You* (Peterson's Guides), *The Effect of Financial Aid Policies on Admission and Enrollment* (The College Board), *Working Together: A Cooperation between Admissions and Financial Aid Offices* (The College Board), and *Shaping the College Experience Outside the Classroom* (University of Rochester Press).

Kathy's special area of expertise is in developing strategic financial aid and retention programs designed to enhance enrollment and net tuition revenue results. A former associate vice president at the University of Rochester and director of financial aid at Earlham College, she pays special attention to ensuring that the solutions recommended are practical, detailed, and implementable. Kathy contributes regularly to *University Business*, authored a chapter titled "The Changing Role of Financial Aid and Enrollment Management" in *New Directions for Student Services* (Jossey-Bass), and regularly speaks at national conferences and seminars such as The National Association of College and University Business Officers, NACAC, and Council of Independent Colleges.

Let's turn the rest of the chapter over to Jim and Kathy. I'll rejoin you in chapter 10, where we'll wrap things up.

Guest Authors:
Jim Scannell and Kathy Kurz

We appreciate your giving us the microphone, so to speak, for what we consider one of the most vital issues facing college recruiters today—the impact of the "New Economic Normal" on college admissions.

Considering the severity of the economic storm we've faced (and we're not out of the woods yet), the question you ask in the chapter introduction is a fair one.

Make no mistake, the economic troubles of 2008 and 2009—known in financial media circles as "the great recession"—have wielded blow after blow to Americans. What's less well known is how colleges have been impacted by the rough-and-tumble economy of the latter part of the first decade of the twenty-first century. And the fact is, different institutions have been impacted in different ways. For the small percentage of institutions that rely heavily on endowment income, the decline in the stock market has created challenges. Granted, although university endowments have fallen in the past few years, they've only fallen 25 percent. During a similar eighteen-month period, by contrast, the U.S. stock market fell over 40 percent. Nevertheless, this decline has meant that even institutions immune to enrollment challenges (like Harvard or Princeton) have had to cut back on spending. Beyond the endowment picture, which significantly impacts only a handful of institutions, there lies an economic "perfect storm" of sorts that has in it enough elements to affect virtually every higher education institution in the country in some way.

The Ingredients of the Storm Include,
But Are Not Limited To…

Decreased state budgets Public colleges and universities pay a heavier price than private ones in times of economic downturn. With tax revenues down, state legislators across the fruited plains are cutting back on higher education budgets, resulting in reduced state allocations. At the same time demand for seats at lower-cost institutions (especially community colleges) is increasing. In addition, many states have significantly reduced state scholarship and grant programs for students. Both public and private institutions, as a result, are faced with the significant challenge of keeping costs affordable with less state financial aid in the package. In fact, one reason many institutions had higher-than-average increases in their financial aid budgets in fall 2009 was that they were stepping in to make up for lost state aid.

Good News, Bad News

Individuals, couples and even businesses have watched as their investments have plummeted during this recession. The College Savings Indicator study conducted by Fidelity Investments in 2008 revealed that parents of high-school-age children have seen their college savings plummet by almost 27 percent. In 2008, parents reported they could pay for approximately 15 percent of their child's college costs, while in 2009 parents were able to cover only about 11 percent.

The good news is that more parents are saving for college than ever before and the amount parents are saving seems to be growing. Last year approximately 60 percent of parents surveyed had saved for their child's college education. In 2009, 63 percent of parents surveyed had a college savings account of some sort. This group of parents can cover approximately 18 percent of their child's college expenses, while parents that invested in 529 plans can cover 36 percent of the total college costs.

A harsher credit environment Banks and other creditors have turned off the lending spigots, meaning that it's much more difficult for families as well as institutions of higher learning to get credit that might help plug some funding gaps. In addition, thanks to new federal regulations surrounding preferred lender lists, many colleges and university aid offices are no longer providing advice to students about where they can find the best financing "deal."

No wiggle room for higher tuition rates It's a catch-22 for college presidents—they need revenue, but the state of the economy is in such disrepair and American families are hurting so badly that colleges can't count on higher rate increases to fill budget gaps.

Increasingly price-sensitive U.S. families With the unemployment rate above 10 percent as we researched and wrote this chapter, the Great American Consumer is on the sidelines, shelving his gilded dreams in favor of lying low until the economic storm clouds pass. We've moved from an economic mindset that favored quality and premium to one that now genuflects to value and thrift. Financial aid officers across the country reported significant increases in the percent of their students applying for financial aid; increases in need

Colleges, Financial Aid under Pressure

According to a study posted on the academic website Student Lending Analytics, more and more colleges are feeling the pinch from increased demand for more financial aid.

In a recent survey of 212 financial aid officers at colleges and universities across the United States, the study found the following:

■ Sixty-nine percent of survey respondents indicated that they had seen an increase in the number of financial aid requests for 2008–9.

■ Two-year public colleges reported the largest increase in financial aid requests with 60 percent of respondents indicating that requests were up over 10 percent on a year-over-year basis.

that exceeded increases in charges; and a spike in the volume of appeals. Look for all these trends to continue next year into 2011 and beyond.

Tougher competition There's been a big ramp-up in *for-profit* colleges like DeVry and Kaplan Career Institute, and they've done a good job of taking the customer-focused tenets of private business and plugging them into college marketing. This is causing traditional schools to give ground, yield-wise, to for-profit colleges. Beyond this, more families are considering community colleges for the first two years of a four-year degree, and competition between four-year schools has never been more vigorous, as institutions fight to keep their share of a traditional market that, at least in some parts of the country, is shrinking.

The above list is certainly enough to keep collegiate administrators up at night. The key is, what are colleges and universities going to do about it?

A Reactionary Phase

Right out of the gate, some institutions of higher learning are resorting to revenue strategies that would have been unthinkable five or ten years ago.

For instance Reed College in Portland, Oregon, recently moved away from need-blind admissions policies, turning away one hundred needy applicants because the school was running out of financial aid for students. "We had so many of these people [who needed additional aid]," the aid director at Reed College, Leslie Limper, told the *New York Times*. "We had to say, oh my goodness, we can't offer aid to everyone who needs it."

Certainly, need-conscious admissions policies are not new to many institutions. However, finding families who can afford to cover the full sticker price to replace needy students not admitted is becoming increasingly challenging.

Reed is hardly alone. Let's review how some other colleges are coping with the challenging economy.

- San Jose State University was recently forced to deny admission to about 4,000 qualified applicants because of California's woeful economic condition. Many public schools rely on state funds to close budget gaps, but San Jose State received 10 percent less than it needed from the state in 2009. That led the school to cut enrollment from 32,750 in 2008 to 29,750 in 2009.

- Arkansas-based Cox College is giving students a break—no increase in tuition for the most recent academic year. College officials say they made the move because of the lousy economy and because students and families were having a difficult time meeting tuition costs. The college president, Dr. Anne Brett, says they made the decision because of the current economy and because some students have had difficulty getting loans. "We thought we would try to eliminate as many barriers as we could by maintaining our tuition and fees at the same level they were at this year, which is also the same level they were at before, so we've actually held them tight for two years, and, in doing that, we've decided that our goal is we're going to grow through this economy rather than cut our budget through the economy."

- The University of Connecticut is planning to convert some of their dorm rooms from housing two beds to four. A state school, applications were up 5 percent in 2009, and school admissions officers anticipate more in-state kids to opt for UConn because of the lower cost.

Other colleges are cutting academic programs that are not profitable (in the nonprofit sense of that word). A few are either eliminating or not updating their landline phone systems. Many are postponing construction projects and implementing furloughs.

Our take? As colleges deal with a difficult economic situation, they also have an opportunity to think strategically about reshaping their curriculum, student service offerings, and recruitment programs. As White House aide Rahm Emanuel once said, "Never let a good crisis go to waste."

The tough times won't always be with us. And while we'll spend the rest of the chapter talking about some more specific ways colleges can shore up their college admissions efforts in this environment, the new normal, we can take some solace in knowing that it won't be this bad forever. Colleges and universities that take a strategic approach to charting their course through these rough waters will emerge as stronger institutions.

How to Survive, and Even Thrive, During Hard Times

Once you get past theory and over to execution, what strategies work to keep colleges viable and profitable in times of major economic peril? Some immediate steps for admissions and financial aid officers to take to prepare for fall 2010 and beyond include the following:

1. Identifying and tracking key performance metrics to ensure there are no surprises in the fall. Although most institutions are very disciplined about tracking the admissions funnel, a surprising number fail to track the number of aid applicants, average need, and average institutional grant expenditures against prior year figures from the same time period.

2. Ensuring that the institution's sticker price, discount rate, and prestige indicators are in alignment relative to those of competitors. Institutions with high sticker prices and low prestige measures relative to those of competitors typically find they must have higher than sustainable discount rates to compensate for the misalignment.

3. Preparing admissions recruiters to make the case for affordability, value, and career outcomes with proof statements. At many institutions data on the employment or graduate student acceptance rates of recent graduates are extremely limited. Given concerns about price and "return on investment" driven by today's economy, addressing this data gap should be a top priority.

4. Keeping admissions and financial aid staffs on the same page by using net tuition revenue goals as the common denominator. If the admissions office is held accountable for meeting targets for class size while the financial aid office is judged on whether or not they stay within budget, the two offices can end up working at cross purposes with the result that institutional net revenues decline.

5. Using an analytical, rather than anecdotal, approach to adjusting aid policies. Some institutions decide to change merit programs or other aid policies based on what they know a competitor is doing or on how individual students responded to aid offers. While keeping an ear to the ground is important, these stories must be balanced with an analytical examination of how yield rates were impacted by various factors, including, but not limited to, financial aid.

6. Paying attention to all enrollments streams. Understanding how financial aid and other policies and programs (like credit evaluation policies) impact recruitment

of transfers and retention of current students is critical as the competition for freshmen grows ever more intense.

Longer term, however, institutions are going to need to seriously address rising costs. One valuable case study comes from Vermont, home to Middlebury College, which made dramatic commitments to keep itself competitive among elite liberal arts institutions.

To be sure, the Middlebury case is representative of other similarly challenged institutions. In the last twenty years or so, Middlebury has undergone a physical and intellectual renaissance. In that time, the prestigious liberal arts school has added a $47 million science center and a $40 million library, as well as a 2,100-seat hockey arena and apartment-style dorms featuring an environmentally friendly dining hall with rooftop vegetation. Middlebury also dug deep to build a multimillion-dollar cultural center for the school's humanities program. The construction included a multimedia screening room and a twenty-foot-high waterfall in the building's equally lavish lobby.

The timing could not have been worse. According to *Fortune* magazine, which published a review of the construction project and its aftermath, the luxury accommodations proved more than the small school could afford.

"But these flourishes are already starting to feel like artifacts of another era. Middlebury's building boom was underwritten by double-digit endowment returns, generous donations, and, like much of the past decade's conspicuous consumption, record amounts of borrowing. The college's debt ballooned from just $5 million in 1987 to $270 million today."

At first, Middlebury found that student applications were on the rise, and significantly so. From 1997 through 2008, new student applications rose by 43 percent. Said Middlebury's treasurer, Patrick Norton, in an interview with the magazine, "These were major, major construction projects that allowed for world-class faculty to be recruited and for world-class students as well. Our rankings and ratings, if you go by those, exploded. We went from this little regional college to somewhere that's really the place to go."

But then the recession hit, and Middlebury's endowment took a $200 million hit in a one-year period (2008–9). College president Ron Liebowitz, to his credit, immediately set out plans for spending cuts to balance the infrastructure expenditures. Among the cost-cutting measures were the following:

■ pay reductions for high-level administrators

■ a freezing of faculty salaries

- the creation of a voluntary early retirement program

- cuts in numerous student services, including the freshman orientation program

- a reduction in daily meals at the school's new "green" dining hall (it would only be used for special events)

To restate, Middlebury is not alone. As the *Fortune* article notes, schools from the University of Arizona to Harvard are suspending raises, eliminating jobs, or reviewing high-profile construction projects.

Says the article:

> "Institutions never thought about the fact that, if there's a substantial fall in the endowment, we're going to have great cutbacks," says Ronald Ehrenberg, a Cornell University economist who studies higher education. "Especially in the private sector, higher ed has grown by adding new things without taking old things away. There's going to be a lot of soul-searching on campuses around the country, and colleges asking, 'What's essential?'"

How the Economy Is Shaping the Collegiate Admissions Landscape

The economic downturn is affecting the choices that students and their parents make:

Community college enrollment is soaring Studies show that more than 90 percent of community college presidents say enrollments are up from the previous year. Meanwhile, another 86 percent reported an increase in full-time students, according to a survey by the Campus Computing Project.

Students who attend traditional four-year colleges are paying more attention to costs A *Princeton Review* survey shows that about two-thirds of students who applied for college in 2009 said the economic downturn affected their choice of colleges.

Increased reliance on financial aid The Princeton survey also found that students have a "great concern around financial aid," with 85 percent stating that they wouldn't be able to pay for college without it.

Diminished value Colleges probably don't want to admit it, but the economic malaise that has haunted the United States in recent years has, by some measures, diminished the value of a college education.

We know, it sounds like blasphemy. But hear us out. College students who graduate during a recession tend to begin their careers in lower-paying jobs, often outside the area of their academic expertise. That, in turn, forces recent graduates into a spin cycle of sorts, where they change jobs faster and with greater regularity than historical peers who graduated into stronger economies and who are presumably well established (Think of college graduates in strong years, as measured by gross domestic product [GDP]. Years like 1996, 1998, and 2004 come to mind.)

A 2006 study by the National Bureau of Economic Research (NBER) bears this out. That study discovered that college graduates who enter the workforce during a recession face an average 9 percent reduction in annual earnings. It doesn't get better soon, either. The NBER study also shows that those storm clouds don't disappear until roughly ten years after graduation.

We don't want to make too much out the "value" question. After all, study after study shows that college graduates make more money, have more fulfilling careers, and are generally happier than their peers who don't have a college education.

All we're saying is that the value question is another potential factor working against colleges and universities trying to gain a solid foothold during a brutal economic period in U.S. history.

Inside Stuff: What the Professionals Are Saying about College Finances and the Economy

Here are some other perspectives on how colleges can adapt to a fast-changing economic landscape from some of the brightest minds in the business.

Jane Wellman is the executive director of the Delta Project on Postsecondary Costs, a nonprofit research organization.

> Can colleges cut their costs, without harming quality or reducing access to students?

> Where should they look to do that? There are four basic areas: First, start with administration, operations and maintenance. Administrative costs have been rising faster than academic program costs for the last decade. Colleges can achieve savings through attention to back-office functions, through consolidated purchasing, improvements in energy efficiency and by holding the line on spending for administrators.

> Second, consolidate programs by eliminating high cost and low demand ones. Every college has high-cost, under-enrolled programs that are not

critical for future community or work force needs. These programs should be eliminated or, if they are essential, consolidated and shared between campuses and made accessible through distance learning.

Third, reduce the costs of producing degrees by cutting out excess units and decreasing student attrition. Most students take far more than the 120 units required for the bachelor's degree. Improving advising and course scheduling and getting rid of excess credits reduces the costs to institutions and to students. The unit cost of degree production can be reduced by getting more students through to the degree.

The majority of colleges have graduation rates below 60 percent—far too low if we are to increase attainment levels. Attrition is a particularly costly problem in graduate education, where unit costs are high and the time it takes to get a degree is way too long, especially when fewer than 50 percent of students are completing degrees.

Finally, too many states have campuses with low enrollments and high costs because they have not grown to scale. These are politically difficult to eliminate and represent important economic and cultural assets to their communities. Still, in this environment, nothing is sacred, and if these facilities can't be made to be economically viable, they should be consolidated or closed. (Room for Debate Blog/ *New York Times,* June 19, 2009)

Cindy Hong is a 2009 graduate of Princeton University, where she majored in public and international affairs. She was a columnist for the *Daily Princetonian.*

In the midst of the recession, universities need to cut down on superfluous student services while maintaining academic needs. During the *bubble* years, super-wealthy universities lured students in with their large endowments. The idea was that these schools offered the best financial aid, the best academic resources and the best campus life. In addition to fantastic libraries, no-loan grants and summer funding for unpaid internships, we also enjoy small perks like free laundry, free food at college sponsored "study breaks" and free concerts.

Though academic expenses are often the most costly, they are also the most essential part of a university. These expenses are not short-term costs on a university balance sheet, but long-term investments for the intellectual growth of its students. Buildings that house larger lecture halls and classrooms will educate students for years to come; departmental funding will support humanities courses that ask students to question values and meanings in life.

Instead, wealthy universities should cut gratuitous student life services. These services are usually viewed as a small price to pay to promote spirit and unity among undergraduate students; they are often poorly attended and over budgeted. Though $100 saved here and $100 saved there don't add up to much, there is an additional benefit. In the absence of organized study breaks and free laundry, students may learn to be more self-sufficient—an important recession-survival skill. (Room for Debate Blog/*New York Times*, June 19, 2009)

Robert Zemsky is the chairman of the Learning Alliance at the University of Pennsylvania.

Despite the public's willingness to tell pollsters they are shocked and dismayed by the unchecked increase in the price of a college education, when the time comes to send their sons and daughters to college, most families shop up, almost uniformly choosing the higher-price option. Students as well as faculty want the prestige money buys having understood that they are more likely to get what they want from an institution that is adding rather than cutting costs.

From these 30 years of false promises I have extracted two basic lessons. First, no one is going to make higher education more efficient one institution at a time. There is neither market nor academic advantage to trying to do with less while every one else is doing with more. What is required is a system solution, one that brings change to all of higher education simultaneously.

Second, making higher education more efficient requires a fundamental change in the production functions that shape higher education's instructional programs. And that means changing what faculty do, when and where they do it, and the time it takes both faculty and students to complete their assigned tasks. My horse in this race is making the three-year baccalaureate degree the standard across all American higher education. (Room for Debate Blog/*New York Times*, June 19, 2009)

Changing College Dreams

A 2009 survey by NACAC, which included responses of 658 high schools and 402 colleges, found the following:

- Seventy-one percent of high school guidance counselors saw an increase in the number of students who chose less-expensive colleges over their "dream school."

- Sixty percent of respondents reported a rise in the number of students planning to enroll in public versus private colleges compared to 2008.

- Thirty-seven percent saw an increase in the number of students planning to enroll in community colleges instead of four-year institutions.

- Fifteen percent reported delaying college due to financial reasons.

- Public college enrollment increased at nearly twice the rate of private schools (47 percent vs. 26 percent).

- Sixty-two percent of private colleges experienced an increase in student transfers out to other schools due to financial hardship.

- Ninety percent of incoming freshmen requested financial aid.

"The potential effects of the economy loomed large over this admission cycle," stated Joyce Smith, NACAC chief executive officer. "It appears that students and families were more concerned about cost, and plans about whether or where to enroll were changed as a result. The colleges' experience this year is more difficult to generalize, though budget cuts and declining yield rates are indicative of a tougher year at many institutions."

Change Is the Challenge—and the Solution

Creativity, vision, discipline, and a commitment to change will see colleges through hard economic times, not an easy assignment for many where status quo has ruled.

Above all, while things will get better economically (they always have), we believe that we have shifted to a new plateau for college admissions and financial aid professionals. Even when the economy turns around, students and families will continue to place more emphasis on value and return on their higher education investment. They will continue to question rising higher education costs and avoid amenities that they don't see as critical.

The one constant? As Brian Niles has been saying all along inside these pages, change isn't a luxury.

It's a necessity.

Chapter 9: The Economy

Conduct price and prestige benchmarking against five of your real competitors (the schools you overlap with for admitted students).

Institution	Price	Perceived Prestige (lower, higher, same)
Your College	$_____	
1. _____	$_____	_____
2. _____	$_____	_____
3. _____	$_____	_____
4. _____	$_____	_____
5. _____	$_____	_____

Do you currently make the case for affordability? Which of the following are part of your planning and recruitment efforts?

❑ Net price calculator ❑ Financial aid case studies

❑ Merit guarantees ❑ Training for admissions staff on financial aid and financing issues

❑ Income distributions for entering cohorts ,

Do you have a contingency plan should state aid be cut? ❑ Yes ❑ No

Do you have a plan in place to recruit and accommodate the growing number of transfer students, including:

❑ improving credit evaluation policies?

❑ forming or maintaining articulation agreements with key feeder community colleges?

❑ clearly explaining the credits transfers will need to complete their degree?

❑ providing support services for transfer students (housing, financial aid programs, special communication stream)?

10

The Future

If you're not confused, you're not paying attention.
—Tom Peters

I'd like to open this, the closing chapter of our book (actually, it's more like a post-script), by focusing not on what has transpired in college admissions or even on what is happening now.

Instead, I'd like to focus on what really counts—the future.

As you'll soon see, I've had a lot of help in mapping out a picture of what that future might look like, but let's lay out a few caveats first.

We're not offering any silver bullets in this book. We recognize that all colleges are different, all students are different, and thus all college admissions programs are different. Just because Alfred University has a special admissions program catered to its specific needs doesn't mean you should copy them.

That said, it is vitally important that we should all be planning for the change that's already under way.

Because, believe me, nobody has all the answers.

Let me tell you a story. My predecessor at La Salle University was Lou Eccleston—a man who had a lot of success helping Michael Bloomberg create Bloomberg Financial and later to became the managing director of the global financial information firm. I went up to New York City one day back in the mid 1990s to talk to him about applying some of his business acumen to La Salle.

Specifically, I wanted to know how Bloomberg Financial operated during major periods of change and if Lou had any relevant advice about what La Salle could do to distinguish itself in such a competitive, part-time MBA marketplace in Philadelphia. (There are over eighty colleges and universities in the greater Philadelphia marketplace.) Lou told me that Dow Jones was Bloomberg's main competition. "But you know what I do?" he asked me when I sat down with him that day. "I ignore them. What if they're doing something wrong?"

He continued: "Instead, I look at what's ahead, add in some 'gut' instinct, and create what I think is right."

It was an eye-opening response. I soon realized it was the same for colleges, which, like Bloomberg Financial, need to be authentic and different in order to succeed. I also realized that looking at your competitors serves only to color your perspective—and not anyone else's. At worst, that self-perspective only makes many college admissions officials copy what their peer institutions are doing—and thus continue to the propagate the "me too" mentality and product offering many institutions have inflicted upon themselves.

How Long Does It Take to Transform Dead Culture?

Lou didn't have all the answers that day and neither do we, but changing the "dead" patterns of admissions departments of colleges and universities might not take as long as we think.

According to my good friend Bob Johnson, president of Bob Johnson Consulting, LLC, economic conditions have likely rendered one of the final death blows throughout higher ed, though many are still reluctant to face this reality. Here's his answer to a simple, yet critical question.

> How long does it take to transform dead culture? It can take a very long time, but perhaps not forever.

> Sure, a serious economic crisis can increase the pace of change, and that's been happening in higher education since 2007. Economic resources are shrinking. Nearly all states are reducing financing for public universities. Private sector schools struggle to maintain enrollments in the face of rising tuition discount rates that averaged more than 40 percent for the entering class in 2009.

> An old culture based on constant growth is breaking everywhere. Higher education has grown almost without check since the baby boomers hit college in the 1960s. Now it is contracting in almost every sector.

Everything that we can expect to continue between now and 2020 is under way.

■ Public universities will reduce the number of majors offered, no matter the outrage of faculty who insist that their programs are essential to preserving civilization as we know it. When resources are scarce, it makes great sense to reduce course offerings in academic programs that graduate very few students.

■ Resistance to loans as part of a financial aid package will continue to have a severe impact on private sector schools. Debt is out of favor. Enrollments at most schools will fall simply because fewer people are willing to take on the debt needed to attend them. Marketing the "value proposition" even more strongly than in the past will not prevent this.

■ Education will become more openly career oriented because that's what people who invest in bachelor's and master's degrees will expect it to provide: access to careers. Successful higher education marketing will focus less on lofty brand claims and much more, at long last, on the outcomes of recent graduates.

■ Community colleges will offer far more bachelor's programs than they do now, overcoming opposition from within higher education to do that. Four-year programs that are important to local communities will be available at low cost because average faculty teaching loads will be higher. This sector will grow.

■ Online learning will continue to increase, especially among people who are considered "traditional" age students. Total higher education enrollment will expand over the next ten years, but little if any of that expansion will happen in the "traditional" residential format.

A piece of the "we must have our money" culture died in Michigan in April 2010. Eastern Michigan University, one of four large regional universities in the state, announced that it would not increase tuition and fees in September 2010, despite reduced state support. It will live on a reduced-calorie diet.

The culture of empire building in higher education is dead. Grand marketing agendas designed to support such empires will die as well.

What Admissions Officers Have to Say About Tough Economic Times

Recently, I participated in a round-table symposium with some of my friends from TargetX along with more than 120 senior college admissions officers from across the United States in Baltimore.

The symposium was supposed to be wide open. But it quickly turned into a free-wheeling discussion about the recession and the economic impact it was having on college admissions departments. There was also dialogue about how the college recruiting market was changing, and not necessarily for the better.

I recall thinking how much anxiety, and even fear, was in the voices of the admissions professionals who had their say that day in Baltimore. Sure, there was plenty of nervous laughter coming from one tale of woe after another, but it was, upon reflection, whistling-past-the-graveyard, gallows-type humor.

I took some rough notes during and after the discussion, and I wound up with the recurring themes listed below when I was done. See if they all don't follow the same trail of anxiety, uncertainty and—very definitely—rampant change that was on the doorstep before anyone was ready for it. But also see more than a hint of defiance from a group of professionals who weren't about to let a major economic downturn beat them.

- We are at a tipping point in higher education. However, opportunity and crisis often go hand in hand (an old Chinese proverb, evidently).

- Colleges can justify their high costs, but only if they have the right conversation with their students.

- Step one, emphasize value. Think about it: for $150 a night over four years, plus a college education, it's a pretty good deal. Colleges need to focus on return on investment—what students and families are getting for their investment.

- Colleges have to reinvent themselves (like Baltimore did with the Inner Harbor, Camden Yards, and the aquarium).

- What are colleges doing about affordability? This is a particularly relevant question, as some students are going into the military to defray costs. Many institutions, on their part, have increased commitment to financial aid this year. But is that investment sustainable? Look behind the admissions curtain, where they are lowering financial aid amounts. Some colleges are even talking about three-year programs.

- Students still want a four-year degree, but they're looking to keep costs down by starting with two-year community colleges then "graduating" to brand-name colleges.

- Some colleges are playing with consortiums—sharing resources is a big part of the "new normal."

- College admissions officers believe they have no control over costs; they feel they "have to make do with what we have." They also feel like they are working harder and getting nowhere fast.

- Moving career services and enrollment offices together is one cost-saving trend.

- College admissions officers feel like they're in a battle with college financial decision-makers. The crux of the problem? Schools are raising tuition rates but offering less financial aid.

- You will see colleges move away from "keeping up with Joneses." No more apartment-style living, gourmet dining halls, or climbing walls. They are "unsustainable" (there's that term again).

- New emphasis: talk about what you do that is unique—that's the key. Otherwise, you will be treated like a commodity, where price dominates. In our publications, we have to rethink the story we are telling: How are we different? Who are we?

- Virginia Commonwealth has 32,000 students and 80 percent of them work while attending college to help pay for it. "The economics of this just does not make sense," said Bill Royall of Royall and Company. "As college leaders see students working outside the classroom, they know we will have to change."

- Colleges can change. After World War II, colleges took in millions of veterans. After Sputnik in 1957, colleges stepped up science and math themes. The lesson? Change is unavoidable—so embrace it.

- For-profit schools offer valuable lessons to traditional colleges—they offer classes when students want them and where they want them. Also, students (or would-be students) can get a for-profit customer service rep on the phone right away—even after 5 PM. Most college admissions offices close at 5 PM.

The big takeaway from that eye-opening morning in Baltimore is this: like Martin Luther King once said, colleges face "the fierce urgency of now."

Where Does the Future Take Us?

Because no vision of the future would be complete without the forward-looking ideas of my co-workers, colleagues, clients, and some of the best admissions professionals in the land, while writing the final chapter of this book I sent out a note asking the people I trust most the following question: "Where do you see the future of college admissions going?"

I think the answers will inform and surprise you. So let's end the book with a taste of the college admissions future, with "a little help from my friends."

Christopher Lydon, Providence College

Authenticity, transparency, and good storytelling will continue to increase as vital components of a successful student recruitment program. However, institutions that can ensure that their current students are satisfied with their experiences will also experience enrollment success by improving retention.

How many institutions devote as much of their resources to retention-related strategies as they devote to their recruitment-related strategies? The future higher education landscape, dominated by price- and return-on-investment-oriented consumers, will be brightest for institutions that devote as much attention to the experiences of the students who are already enrolled as they do to marketing to their prospective students.

The best storytellers are those satisfied by their experiences. Exceed current student expectations and provide them with opportunities to touch your future storytellers.

Ray Ulmer, Vice President, Marketing, TargetX

Any look into the future of college admissions should include a look back to September 2008 when TargetX brought together 150 enrollment officers for the first "iThink" discussion. Moderator Jeff Kallay asked them, "Where do you see college admissions in five years?" Here are some of the predictions:

- Schools will be closing doors.

- The federal government will be more involved.

- Panic at some institutions will lead to unsavory admissions practices.

- More proprietary institutions.

- A retreat from so much e-marketing to a more personal approach.

- Students will be admitted at the end of their junior year.

- Discussions about whether "fit" still matters when cost is so critical.

- There will not be enough students to go around.

- Conversations with eighth graders and their parents.

- Back to basics—less Web 2.0.

- Greater control by students in developing their own programs.

- Yield keeps going down, melt keeps going up.

- More business leaders becoming presidents at colleges and universities.

Barbara Elliott, University of the Arts

In the future successful student recruitment will be high tech and high touch and will require greater collaboration. It will become increasingly important to develop a relationship with the prospective student, and his or her family, early in their secondary school years.

Greater collaboration and planning between the admissions and institutional communication offices will be critical. The institution will need to build a presence in the minds of the prospective student, the family, and those who influence them. This can't be accomplished through a "student" recruitment effort alone.

Increased pressure on institutional resources will require carefully choreographed activities that allow for cross-fertilization of the populations that the institution traditionally cultivates. Events once targeted individually to enrolled students, alumni, and new students may merge. Campaigns for each of these populations will be redesigned so that, with slight modification, they can be directed at multiple audiences and provide an institutional message reinforced through multiple channels. CRM capabilities of websites will push personalized information to specific audiences, all emanating from a single source within the university's communications operations.

Admissions professionals will devote an even greater percentage of time to providing personal access to students and families. More conversation and more authentic person-to-person touch points will be critical as technology and binary personalization become even more pervasive in daily life.

Jodi Bailey, Alfred University

The first form of education came through storytellers. The storytellers were revered among their people for passing on history, religion, skills, and so forth.

We must all get back to storytelling. Students and their parents need to be able to envision themselves on our campuses doing what our students are doing. If they can't see themselves there, they need to be looking elsewhere. That said, storytelling is not an easy feat. It must be authentic to the institution and students there. It isn't just standing and sharing your story in front of a group. Storytelling now must be done in a carefully constructed communications plan that includes print and electronic media—the options for which are beginning to be endless.

Jim DeSanto, Implementation Specialist, TargetX

Full disclosure: I'm the new guy at TargetX without as much admissions experience as some of the others at TargetX. What I do have are two younger siblings who are going through the college admissions process right now. So my response here is based entirely on what I've observed over the past two years.

I think the future of college admissions boils down to one thing: getting past fear. Getting past the fear of not doing what worked in the past. Getting past the fear of trying new things on your campus.

High school students are bombarded in their daily lives with mass marketing that has taught them to not trust anything they haven't discovered for themselves.

This is why it is more important than ever to really cultivate and nurture relationships with students who are truly seeking information about your school. Prospects are looking for a personal connection that they themselves initiate. But it can't all hinge on print campaigns done the same old way. Do you open your junk mail? Why would an eighteen-year-old?

Here's an example of a recent conversation with my sister (a high school senior):

Me: Hey Sister, You starting to narrow down your short list?

Sister: Yeah, I guess.

Me: That's a ton of mail from schools—you planning on visiting any of them?

Sister: Nope…. But I am going to [insert school name] next week.

Me: That's cool… did they send you something?

Sister: No… they called me on my birthday, which you forgot to do by the way. And this girl from the softball team friended me, too.

For my sister, the opportunity to talk to a current student online combined with a personal touch from the admissions office were all she needed. Next up will be her campus visit experience—always the "make-or-break" point from what I've seen so far.

Don't be afraid.

Chris Walters, Penn State University

The first admissions officers held other responsibilities and thus were overseeing admissions only part-time. Can you imagine?

Fifteen years ago, the personal touches from admissions offices were done only by the small private colleges that didn't have the name recognition of their larger public counterparts. Today, there are very few—if any—college admissions offices simply sitting back with the "build it and they will come" mind-set. The transformation and specialization of college admissions offices is nothing short of spectacular. Technology has been instrumental in this transformation and that's not going away.

I see the future of college admissions as a blending of old ideas produced with new technology that will allow for even greater personalization and faster processes. Instead of faculty picking up the phone to call prospective students in their discipline, we'll be able to beam a message into their homes with a thirty-second promotion of study options. Campus tours will be done with hover scooters and nobody will need to walk backward. And admissions applications will load automatically from an iPhone app into our systems for immediate decisions.

The really old-school was a much simpler time, but without these specializations, we go back to one part-time admission person…can you imagine?

Lori Mann, Biola University

Disclaimer: I think good ideas are meant to be molded and reconfigured to turn them into more good ideas, and even great ideas. Therefore I give credit for some of this content to Dr. John Mark Reynolds, associate professor of philosophy at Biola's Talbot School of Theology.

My perspective on admissions relates to graduate students, the growing market of adult learners who don't fall into neat categories nearly so much as undergrads. They pretty much know what they want, and are looking for personal <u>and</u> practical ways to get their education. That's why graduate admissions will become less about the university's brand and more about the professors who teach at that university. Professors will become their own brand.

Differentiation among programs for a grad student will be to find a school with a scholar with whom they want to work. Between decent school A with a scholar whose work fascinates them and better school B with only the "name," they will choose A if the scholar gives any indication he or she might want to work with them.

This also means that grad students will take classes from the profs they want regardless of the university with which they are affiliated. Thus, admissions becomes decentralized, featuring self-service "matching services" to connect students to profs rather than to schools.

Grad students won't want to go into debt unless it is in a profession and from a school with a track record of grads being able to pay off debt fast. (See UCLA's medical school.) Financial resources will be better spent on scholarships and grants so universities will finally rethink their budgeting priorities.

Last and not least, community will always count and loneliness can ruin a grad school experience. Alumni will become a more important source of finding community for those considering a move for graduate school.

Jeff Kallay, Vice President, Consulting, TargetX

The future is now.

Colleges and universities must embrace transparency and authenticity. That means being comfortable in their own skin as well as knowing and stressing the ways in which they are unique. I've visited hundreds of schools and find that most are obsessed with the school up the road or with presenting a version of themselves that isn't real. I've heard countless presidents say, "We want to be the Harvard of [insert geographical reference]. Why can't they just be their own school?

Schools must also embrace authenticity and render their true selves to prospective families. If you're a quirky liberal school, be that, own it. If you're a conservative neofascist campus, own it.

To survive in the future you can't be all things to all people. Schools must draw a line in the sand.

Millennials crave authenticity. They cherish faults and differences. Show yours.

The future belongs to those who are confident to be who they are.

America is moving toward "café experiences." We want customization and authenticity, as well as unique and personal interaction.

Sam Mahra, Southern New Hampshire University

I think the whole concept of enrollment management is changing when the "courtship" of a student continues until the time they enroll.

Students today are more technology savvy than any other generation before them. How we communicate with students needs to evolve as well. I still feel that some colleges and universities have adapted slowly, with many over-relying on tele-counseling and print mailings to attract bright minds. Utilization of social media is one of many methods that colleges are using to stay in front of prospective students.

First, today's college-bound student shops for colleges and universities similar to the way a consumer shops for products on the Internet. More often than not, the first visit is a virtual one. The virtual visit is an experience that allows prospective students complete and anonymous control. This experience can also be tailored to their interests and overcome geographic boundaries.

Therefore, websites and any other form of electronic media must be able to articulate core value propositions of an institution that answer, "What's in it for me?"

Secondly, I also feel that more institutions will adapt business models that are identical to those in the for-profit college sector. In the for-profit sector, communication is instant, where the first school to respond to a student's needs usually ends up the winner.

The most progressive institutions have seen the success the for-profit sector has achieved with online learning and the continuing education marketplace. Traditional universities and colleges benefit from borrowing a business model without the negative aspects that come with for-profit education.

These models will force institutions to challenge their notions of what enrollment management should be. Moving forward, I think we will see the traditional enrollment management structure change where recruitment and retention are two separate functions. I envision two separate structures, where there is a student recruitment and marketing division that is separate from a retention division, as the competition for attracting students increases.

Third, many parents and families are combining campus visits with their traditional family vacations. I think that most universities will move away from the "cookie-cutter" campus tour of stating facts and looking at buildings. While that is important, facts will be need to balanced with storytelling and anecdotes that establish a relationship with the prospective student.

Institutions need to invest not only in resources but in their tour guides, who may serve as the only point of contact between a prospect and the institution. How many of us have heard of an awful campus tour because the guide lacked the appropriate level of presentation and information? Having highly trained tour guides who can develop a relationship with their audience is more important than any gimmick or gift an institution may provide.

In conclusion, the ideas presented here will require institutions to challenge traditions and the status quo. Only colleges and universities that are true to the spirit of learning and innovation will be the ones that prosper.

Bruce Exstrom, Alleghany College

Students of tomorrow require information at their fingertips now. Instant communication is critical, and part of the communication is the personal touch. The decision about where and how to attend higher learning institutions is complex and will continue to be a life-changing event. Students want career guidance and we need to answer the question "Why is your college relevant?" Access via a wide range of technology must be available, from a simple telephone call or a personal visit to talk to social networks and our own websites. We must respond to the needs of students and control information that is shared when possible. Social networks allow for anyone to post information; we must be cognizant of the information out in cyberspace and work to manage our flow of information. Admissions is a challenge, it is important, it is critical to our future sustainability, and it is not an afterthought. We have an obligation to reach prospective students; we can change their lives and offer opportunity.

G. Edward Hughes, Kentucky Community College

The future is not admissions and recruitment or enrollment management from the college to the student. In the future, the colleges will be recruited by students based on the products the colleges offer. The savvy colleges will find ways to engage students and build personal relationships using the students' own networks and based on the students' profiles, not unlike the Internet marketing strategies employed by Amazon, Netflix and iTunes.

Jeremy Spencer, Alfred University

The future is clear: enrollment managers' importance will grow within institutional leadership, thus requiring a bigger "seat" within the presidential cabinet. The issue I foresee is whether or not the current crop of middle managers (i.e., assistant and associate directors) will be interested in tackling the issues or dealing with the stressors presented at the vice-presidential level. If professionals with admissions backgrounds aren't willing to rise to the occasion, the void will be filled with professionals with more of a corporate orientation. This shift may create a rip in the very fabric that undergirds the NACAC's "Statement of Principles of Good Practice" and the collaborative way in which college admissions officers relate to each other while recruiting students to their respective schools. We need experienced admissions professionals to guide us through the changing economic climate and ensure that core admissions philosophies aren't lost as institutions grapple with ways to remain viable in the educational marketplace.

John Matechen, Douglas Education Center

The future will depend on what the school has to offer the student. The "quality of education" provided by a school is not a special attribute that is a differentiating factor or unique marketing tool. It is simply the ante that keeps us in the game and what a student expects. What will be expected in the future, in fact the very near future is collaboration between admissions and career services working together to establish a strong relationship with students that is well beyond the classroom and focused on their desire to enter the workplace.

Wes Waggoner, Texas Christian University

Higher education is becoming an increasingly market-driven economy. Academic divisions respond to the desire for career-oriented, specialized majors (e.g., forensics). Housing and dining offices build suites and apartments with the comforts of home and hotel; meal plans offer seemingly unlimited variety and availability. Families expect it, particularly at institutions that charge premium tuition, be they private or public.

In recruiting, the availability of information has been defined by the World Wide Web—day or night—type http://www.***.edu and presto! You have what you need. Admissions offices have realized the need for a 24/7 presence of information, and I see the future demanding expansion. Already, regional representatives are in cities to provide access to personalized conversations beyond the one week of college fairs when most colleges are visiting a city. Prospective students visit campus at all times, not just 8–5, Monday through Friday. Recruiting in the future must allow students to have a personal, individualized, authentic experience whenever they set foot on campus.

The phrase "We're closed on Saturday and Sunday" no longer works in retail, and it's not likely to last very long in the nonprofit, educational industry either. To serve our students, we'll be there whenever we need to be there.

James Winterstein, National University of Health Sciences

Crystal gazing is like shadow gazing—one might get lucky and come out right, but then again…

The reality is that we don't know what the future holds with any certainty, and that has become more and more clear with the current political and economic climate. I have a good friend who is a futurist with excellent outcomes, but he says "current conditions predict future trends," and based on the current conditions, the future trends don't look good. Personally, I think this is something we academicians must look at very closely.

We are, in the short term, often blessed with increased admissions during a recession as people take the opportunity to retrain, but if the economic depression is long term, quite the opposite will be true. That being said, I look at the current economic circumstances and recognize the enormous debt that is being created currently and realize that unless private industry in the United States is capable of developing globally needed products, services, or ideas that can generate a massive influx of wealth to the United States, the current debt will drag us down for decades to come—and that will mean poor admissions statistics.

I dislike being pessimistic and by nature I am not, but at times realism rises to the top and must be acknowledged. Once acknowledged, however, what do we do that could make a difference? We need to provide a product that will function as a generator of value to the individual as well as to the country. To that end, admissions must be demanding and once a person is admitted, our responsibility should be toward providing whatever assistance is needed to increase the chances of success.

We need to be innovative with the technology that is available and that which will become available while not forsaking the essential personal interaction that has been the hallmark of the educational process since antiquity.

Is the future for college admissions bright? I believe it can be, but more likely it is a light at the end of a tunnel. We must use this time well so that when we emerge again into that light, we have a far better educational plan in place that will provide us with leaders who serve for more altruistic reasons.

Vickie Adkison, Kennesaw State University

I, too, believe the future is now.

While we need to continue using whatever new media and technology are available to us, we also need to continue to be "old-fashioned" as far as having an open door policy with our admissions officers being available to talk with parents and students on a walk-in basis. Parents, more than students, want that extra coddling and one-on-one attention and the security that may come with putting a name with a face and having access to someone they feel they can call when they have questions regarding our university.

Our school is growing more and more every year and we have to stay on top of all of the new things we have to offer prospective students. I will continue to believe the best marketing tool we have is the currently enrolled student. These students make the best tour guides because they can speak from personal experience.

We will continue to make prospective students feel important to us using correspondence via personalized messages, photos, and thank-you notes after they have visited our university. We will continue to use College Board and other tools available to us as a database for us to "mine" students that fit a variety of specialized programs that KSU offers.

Marianne Inman, Central Methodist University

College admissions will continue to be highly competitive. Colleges and universities will need to differentiate themselves in ways that matter to students and their families and in ways that they can authentically deliver.

Students of today and tomorrow are seeking flexibility, convenience, quality, opportunity, and ultimately the credential. They are also concerned about cost and about obtaining the best value for their money. This does not necessarily mean that low cost always trumps higher cost but that students need to feel they are getting what—if not more than—they are paying for.

Because of the large number of postsecondary opportunities available to students, aggressive and targeted marketing will continue. The extensive use of technology will continue. The personal touch will be increasingly important. Colleges and universities are often criticized for their seemingly high costs, yet the programs, services, and facilities that students and their families expect and demand drive up those costs. I do not see a "no frills" degree becoming widely popular any time soon, and thus cost and affordability will continue to be challenges that institutions must address.

The admissions world will continue to be exciting, for the task of enrollment professionals is to find the best match between students and institutions. The diversity of colleges and universities and their mission to serve learners of all ages and interests are the basis for the strength and popularity of American higher education.

Annemarie Nagle, Marketing Manager, TargetX

Technology use in college admissions will continue to increase.

Some people believe (or hope) that things will go "back to basics," but that's just not possible. We are in an era of interactive, interconnected admissions and the evolution of technology will only continue to amaze us. Admissions offices will continue to direct more efforts toward using technology effectively and our communication plans will forever be changed. Opportunities to engage and interact outside the campus visit will become more prevalent to students in the planning process.

Our target audience will also become younger.

Communications will become heavier in the freshman and sophomore years. Younger students will begin receiving more college information from colleges and universities or they will begin finding it themselves through a variety of channels. Name recognition with a younger audience will become more important in order to build a relationship and cultivate them into your campus community.

Bryn Campbell, University of Delaware

With the shift to the "experience economy," I believe we will see some small but vital shifts in everything we do.

1. Travel season turning into visiting season. While many of us have seen a decrease in the number of students attending our sessions at high schools, we have also seen an increase in overall visitors to our campuses. Add the down economy into the mix and an easy way to save money and work more efficiently means cutting back on travel to schools that "always send us apps."

2. Visiting managers and electronic communication managers as permanent spots in admissions offices. Schools are already starting the trend by giving counselors specific areas of focus based on their skills. But as we see more stealth applicants who want to see campus and do nothing else, we are looking at the creation of specific managers who spend 90 percent of their time or more dedicated to these tasks.

3. More elaborate campus visits that are simpler to run. As Jeff Kallay would say, we all need to find our signature moment. Working with that, we as admissions need to create a campus visit built on that moment, create the memory, and send them on their way. Students no longer need the hand-holding their parents do, and we need to give them what they want in an overstimulated world. I see colleges not being too far off from finding this formula.

4. Fewer admissions talking heads and more time with students and departments. These students are inundated by the media about how this process works—right or wrong, we need to accept that they already think they know it all. Give them the admissions information in a clear, concise way and send them out of that presentation room to experience your campus. What do they need to know that's not on your website?

The hardest part for me to face is the same comment I am guilty of saying on a weekly (if not daily) basis: "Why is higher-ed always ten years behind the curve?" Technologically, socially, and so forth, higher-ed does not keep up with the trends. Welcome to sales. Introduce yourself to social networking but don't be a "creeper"—that old guy who sends you messages but you don't really know who he is. Shorten it up; our Millennial attention spans can't handle long periods of time. And finally, love what you do, because if you don't, these multitasking Millennials and their black hawk parents will drive you crazy. It's only going to get more interesting from here!

Adrienne Bartlett, Vice President, Client Experience, TargetX

I'm hoping to see more schools seriously embrace the idea that "customer service is the new marketing."

Since we know traditional "talk-at" marketing doesn't work the way it used to, delivering exceptional student experiences (from the prospect stage through graduation) has become the most effective way to inspire people to engage with and talk about your brand.

These days, the web provides plenty of places to talk: websites, social networks, blogs, Twitter, message boards, online forums—and that doesn't even cover traditional word-of-mouth (college's oldest form of "marketing").

To me, the future of admissions marketing has to include the commitment of more time and resources toward energizing customers and inspiring them to "evangelize" your brand.

It starts with purposefully designing every experience to exceed expectations. Then it relies on giving enthusiastic brand supporters the tools they need to amplify their messages.

At its core, the whole strategy can be simplified to two steps:

1. Give them something positive to say.

2. Make it easy for them to say it (and share it).

When you provide an experience worth talking about, you don't need to do all of the talking anymore. You can focus on providing helpful content, answering questions, participating in conversations, and solving problems for prospects and families.

For some reason, customer service seems to be a lost art in this down economy (where it's needed most). Set yourself apart in the future by reversing that trend.

Jill Landesberg-Boyle, University of Massachusetts

More and more we are seeing trends that foretell what is next on the horizon.

The first trend is the transition from a vice president for student affairs to a vice president for enrollment management and student affairs (or, in some cases, a vice president for enrollment management in addition to the vice president for student affairs). I believe this trend is in response to a heavier reliance on tuition revenue to balance the budget. As states tighten their belts and restrict the operating revenue they appropriate to their public institutions of higher education, cash-strapped schools are limiting the number of new students they enroll as a means to cut costs or, if they are private institutions that can set their own tuition or colleges whose state funding formula is based on FTE, they can look to student enrollment to help close the budgetary gap left by the state cuts. Since most states also strictly limit tuition raises at their public colleges, the only way to increase tuition revenue is through increasing the numbers of students who are enrolled. Unfortunately, it seems that most schools find it easier to enroll new students than to focus on retention, a much more complicated and multifaceted issue to address effectively.

The second trend is the increase of students entering community colleges. Many of these students are approaching their education planning to move on to the university level after their first two years at the community college. This rise of associate of arts students tends to be driven by the increasing cost of tuition, which universities are typically allowed to increase at a higher level than their community college counterparts in their state, and/or the closing of doors at the universities. Bear in mind that universities do not have a mission of open access, as is the case with community colleges. Therefore, unlike the community colleges, the universities can choose to be more selective as a means of cutting costs. The other role of community colleges, workforce development, also becomes more important as the bulk of jobs that are predicted to open up are not in the high-paying, executive positions but workforce- and vocationally-oriented jobs.

Finally, there has been a proliferation of private, for-profit schools. These schools emphasize enrollment in ways that most public schools have never even considered. Just look at any job list, for example higheredjobs.com or the *Chronicle*, and you will find a multitude of for-profit institutions advertising. While ten years ago it was rare to see for-profit institutions hold such prominence in the job market, today it is commonplace. This tells us that the growth in that industry is significant. There is no doubt that the ideas and practices for-profit schools use to recruit will begin to seep into the public arena and shape our future approach to recruitment.

Chapter 10: The Future

What do you think the greatest challenges will be to your institution in the future?

_____

_____

Are you and your staff taking steps to continuously follow industry changes by:

❑ reading books (targetx.com/shelfari)

❑ sharing pertinent news (targetx.com/delicious)

❑ attending conferences (targetx.com/slideshare)

❑ participating in webinars (Video Library: targetx.com/videos)

❑ following industry blogs and bloggers (targetx.com/ithink)

Given what you read, how would *you* answer the question "Where do you see the future of college admissions going?"

What action steps can you take now to address the enrollment management challenges at your institution (refer to exercise at the end of Chapter 1)?

Issue	Action Step
Cost of attendance	_____
Lack of leadership	_____
Losing funding Sources	_____
Student retention	_____
Quality of students	_____
Resistance to change	_____
Embracing technology	_____

The End

Something has changed within me. Something is not the same. I'm through with playing by the rules of someone else's game. Too late for second-guessing. Too late to go back to sleep. It's time to trust my instincts. Close my eyes and leap!
—Defying Gravity, from the musical *Wicked*

We've come to the end of this journey, and as the Chinese proverb says, "the journey is the reward." It has been a wonderful journey putting together our thoughts, and the thoughts from some of our friends in the industry, in this book. We hope it has stimulated your thinking as to how college recruiting and admissions need to change to help institutions survive in the world ahead.

I would be remiss in not thanking some extraordinary people who have helped pave the path. Over the past twenty years I have come across and been surrounded by some amazing people. They make me think differently, challenge my abilities, challenge my ideas and in the end make me a better person. I have been fortunate to be able to work with some of them every day. And I am honored to call them friends.

The TargetX team is my second family. I thank the universe on a daily basis for conspiring to bring us together.

- Mike Crusi, my business partner and longtime friend who has an extraordinary way of seeing things differently and challenging the status quo and the team, while keeping one eye on the code.

- Ray Ulmer, employee #1, my PR mentor, and one of the kindest people I've ever met.

- Adrienne Bartlett, the "old soul" and guru of all things media (old and new) who has the heart of an angel.

- Jeff Kallay, the most exciting speaker in higher education (and one of the best speakers I've ever heard period) who with a commanding voice and confidence makes you want to change for the better—now!

- Kim Nagy, a beautiful storyteller and keeper of the creative project plan who helped make this effort stay on course.

- Brian O'Connell who has done a wonderful job in crafting our story, bringing it all together in one cohesive tome.

- And a special thank you to Ed Curry, our longtime friend and business guide, who kicked me in the ass to finally write all of this stuff down.

And to the rest of the team—Bob Mootz, Abey Mathews, Tim Ogline, Scott Parks, Kevin Corr, Dara Corrato, Jeff Leisse, Jill Duppler, Trent Gilbert, Vilpesh Mistry, Jim DeSanto, Patrick Kelly, Celesta Brown, Cynthia Ford, Jean Pagnotta, Emily Welsh, Jackie Egitto, Annemarie Nagle and those that will join us in the future—thank you for taking small and large leaps of faith to jump on the bus and share your knowledge, expertise, and passion to help fulfill our vision and values.

Finally to my father, who was only able to read the one chapter we published in the fall of 2009 before passing away in January 2010 from a longtime illness. He was very proud of what we've accomplished at TargetX over the past twelve years and enjoyed watching a business grow and maintain its values and convictions. He has always been my silent guide, even today.

If you are new to higher education or to admissions, my advice to you is to surround yourself with good, caring, decent people like those I've mentioned above. It will make the journey all that more successful, focused, and, perhaps most importantly, fun.

And when you're not sure what's next, close your eyes … and leap!

Best wishes to you. And thank you for your time.

—Brian

Index